D1286584

Costume of Colonial Times

BY

ALICE MORSE EARLE

NEW YORK
EMPIRE STATE BOOK CO.
1924

Republished by Gale Research Company, Book Tower, Detroit, 1974

Library of Congress Cataloging in Publication Data

Earle, Alice (Morse) 1851-1911.
Costume of colonial times.

1. Costume--United States--History. 2. Costume--History--18th century. I. Title.
GT607.E2 1974 391'.00973 75-159946
ISBN 0-8103-3965-X

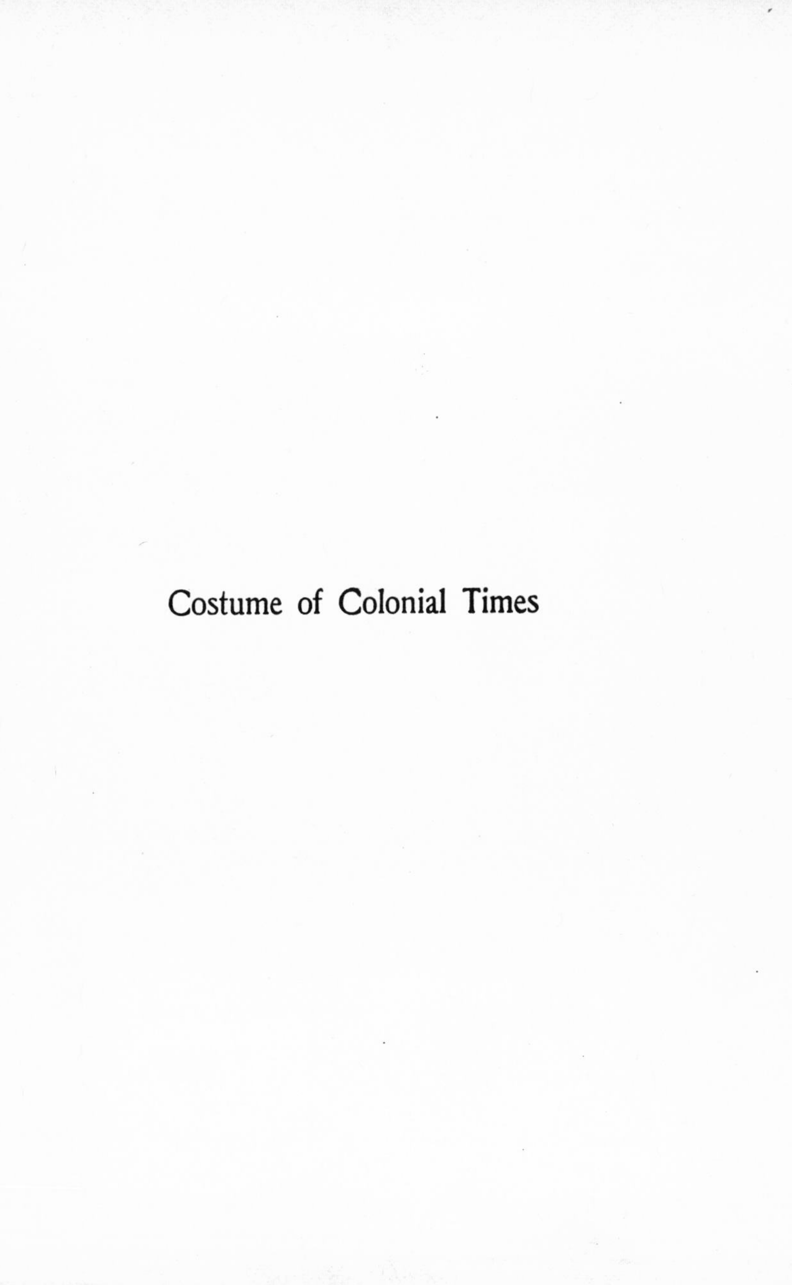

Costume of Colonial Times

TO

HENRY EARLE

CONTENTS

FOREWORD

The material for the compilation of this glossary has been found in old letters, wills, inventories of estates, court records, and in eighteenth-century newspapers, hundreds of which have been carefully examined and noted.

Though the work would appear to have been tedious, it has not so been found. The old letters and wills have the charm of quaint orthography and diction, and also the purely personal interest arising from the sense of touch with the writer thereof, which always appeals so vividly to the imagination. The inventories and court records have been so filled with curious terms and items that they have never seemed monotonous.

Foreword

The advertisements contained in old newspapers have had for me a special charm, the same indescribable and inexplicable fascination that held Hawthorne an eager reader and made him spend hours poring over the dusty files. These advertisements afford an opportunity of insight into the manners of their times no less interesting than valuable, and in them contemporary social life is largely written. Through the many glimpses thus given of curious old-time customs, and the full knowledge obtained of century-old fashions, the reading and transcription has never proved tiresome. I can fully echo Mr. Ashton's declaration that "by taking the very words of people then living, a charm has been lent to the task which fully compensated for the labor."

Though the compilation of this glossary has been a pleasure, I can also say, with truth, in old Sir Thomas Browne's words, "I have studied not for my own sake only, but for theirs that study not for themselves." I hope and believe this book will prove of value and of use to artists, to portrayers of old colonial days—portrayers not only in colors, but in words—and that it will help to prevent in the future any such anachronisms as now disfigure many of our stories and accounts of the dress of early times, not only through incorrect verbal description, but through equally imperfect and inaccurate illustration.

That the value of this work as a book of reference may be complete, I have endeavored to give the price of materials and garments at various dates, especially in early colonial days; also to show when certain attire came into fashion—when it became no longer the vogue.

When I have written of garments or stuffs familiar to us at the present day, it was because there was something in their old-time form or use that varied from that of our own day ; or because some incident of interest was attached to their assumption. Sometimes it was simply to show how ancient in use they were.

In the main, the fashions of the colonies were the fashions of old England ; when a garment or headgear came to be the mode in London, scarce a year elapsed ere Philadelphia, Boston, and Newport gentry were also bedecked therewith. Still this rule had exceptions. When all French and English dames wore "commodes," I do not doubt that women of wealth in New York and Virginia thus dressed their heads, but I have not been able to find a single proof of the fact, not even an instance of the use of the word on this side the Atlantic.

I have found, however, that English authorities on costume have made many errors in dates ; for, of course, no modish garment would be advertised in a New England newspaper eight or ten years be-

fore it was worn in London. I have therefore paid slight heed to modern English and French writers on dress, but have preferred to cite my own examples of the use of words, and to shape my own definitions; I note and define over one hundred terms not given by Planché, the authority on English costume.

The references to New England sources of information may appear to predominate herein, but the records and accounts of the southern colonies have been searched with equal care. Owing, however, to the events of history, especially to the devastation of two wars, the documents and manuscripts, and even the newspapers of Virginia, Maryland, and the Carolinas have not been preserved to the same extent as have been those of the more northern colonies.

To the valuable books of reference in the library of the Long Island Historical Society, and to the priceless files of newspa-

pers in that happy haven for antiquaries—the library of the American Antiquarian Society at Worcester, Mass.—I owe much of the information contained in these pages. To these societies I give my sincere thanks for their unbounded and cordial generosity and their unvarying courtesy.

ALICE MORSE EARLE.

Brooklyn Heights, September, 1894.

History of Colonial Dress

HISTORY OF COLONIAL DRESS

THE most devoted follower of fashion in the present day gives no more heed to dress and the modes than did the early American colonist. This close attention was paid by the settler to his own attire and that of his neighbors, not so much through his vanity or love of fashion and dress, as through his careful regard of social distinctions and his respect for the proprieties of life. He believed that "dress had a moral effect upon the conduct of mankind," and he studied to dress "orderly and well according to the fashion and the time." Dress was also to the colonists an important badge of rank; and for many years class distinctions were as carefully guarded and insisted upon in America as in England. Attempts were made through sumptuary laws in different colonies to definitely fix and restrict the dress of what were deemed the lower classes; laws were passed similar to those which had been enforced in England by the English kings and queens, especially the dress-loving Elizabeth. But these statutes proved a dire failure in the new land, and universal freedom and much diversity of attire became a part of the universal liberty.

Through the various records of colonial days which have been preserved to us, and through the interesting, though ofttimes crude portraits of our ancestors which still exist, it is possible to trace with considerable precision the variations in dress in the different settlements; to note how quickly in some localities the thrifty simplicity of the attire of the early planters was abandoned, and to picture the succession of modes.

The earliest Virginia planters were many of them Cavaliers and had no Puritanical horror of fine dress; hence small attempt was made at restriction of extravagance in attire in that colony. Wealth was great, and if the tobacco crop were large and factors prompt, doubtless the gowns and doublets which were sent from England were correspondingly rich. Some mild sumptuary edicts were sent forth "to suppress excess in cloaths," such as the orders to Sir Francis Wyatt in 1621. He was enjoined "not to permit any but the council and the heads of hundreds to wear gold in their cloaths or to wear silk till they make it themselves." This order was probably intended not so much to discourage the wearing of silk as to encourage its manufacture (as silk culture was for many years a bee in the colonial bonnet), and the law must have been a dead letter. John Pory, Secretary of the Virginia colony, wrote about that time to a friend in England,

> Our cowekeeper here of James citty on Sundays goes accoutred all in ffreshe fflaminge silke, and a wife of one that had in England professed the blacke arte not of a Scholler but of a Collier weares her rough bever hatt with a faire perle hatband, and a silken sute there to correspondent;

which, I must say, strikes me as somewhat grotesque and even comic, when I think of the Indian-surrounded wilderness wherein the "fflaminge silk" and fair pearl hatband were worn.

In 1660 the Virginia colonists were ordered to import "no silke stuffe in garments or in peeces (except for whoods and scarfes), nor silver or gold lace, nor bone lace of silke or threads, nor ribbands wrought with gold or silver in them." I know of no prosecutions or confiscations under this law.

In Maryland, that state of freedom, both religious and social, no attempt was made to restrict the dress of the settlers; and there is evidence that rich and varied wardrobes were brought over by the lords of the manors, those aristocratic emigrants,—more varied and costly dress probably than was that of any Puritans or Quakers. I have never seen in the records of any other colony proofs of such multifariousness of head and neck gear, such frivolities and fripperies as a Maryland gentleman left by will, with other attire, in 1642: "Nine laced stripps, two plain stripps, nine quoifes, one call, eight crosse-cloths, a paire holland sleeves, a paire womens cuffs, nine plaine neck-cloths, five laced neck-cloths, two plaine gorgetts, seven laced gorgetts, three old clouts, five plaine neckhandkerchiefs, two plain shadowes."

In nearly all cases in Maryland and Virginia, the prices of garments and of stuffs by the yard or piece are given in pounds of tobacco. Hence, through the variations in value of that staple, it is difficult now to assign exact values to articles named. Even tailors' bills are made out with tobacco as currency. One of the year 1643 reads:

To making a suit with buttons to it, . .	80 lb.
1 ell canvas, ...	30 "
for dimothy linings, ...	30 "
for buttons & silke, ...	50 "
for points, ...	50 "
for taffeta, ...	58 "
for belly pieces, ...	40 "
for hooks & eies, ...	10 "
for ribbonin for pockets, ...	20 "
for stiffinin for a collar, ...	10 "
Sum, ...	378 lb.

As urban life for the wealthy did not prevail in the eighteenth century in the southern colonies as in New England, New York, and Pennsylvania, but instead segregation on widely separated plantations, there was not through those years the same constant and general rivalry in dress that was seen in the large northern towns. There was exceptional elegance at gatherings at races and fairs and all folk-mootings, even at the courts-leet and courts-baron in Maryland. But at home the planters went in negligée costumes, banians and night caps, as William Byrd notes the ordinary dress in 1735. A writer in the *London Magazine* in 1745 also remarked this carelessness of dress of the Southern planters. He says:

> 'Tis an odd sight, that except some of the very Elevated Sort few Persons wear Perukes, so that you would imagine they were all sick or going to bed; Common People wear Woolen and Yarn Caps, but the better ones wear white Holland or Cotton. Thus they travel fifty miles from Home. It may be cooler for ought I know, but methinks 'tis very ridiculous.

Perhaps no quotation could show more thoroughly than the above the universal prevalence of wig-wearing at that date among folk of any pretence toward being well dressed. Not only gentlemen, but children, servants, negro slaves, soldiers, even convicts, wore false headgear. A shipload of disreputable, indentured servants, who were nearly all rogues and vagabonds, were, ere being landed in America, supplied with second-hand wigs, in order to cut a comparatively respectable figure and obtain positions as schoolmasters—a calling which seemed to gather the worst dregs of the southern colonies, and which was almost always filled by redemptioners. So when the planters could ride in their own hair, and with any such ridiculous headgear as woollen or cotton caps, they were indeed hopelessly lost to any sense of propriety of carriage or dignity of apparel.

The southern newspapers of the half century previous to the Revolution show few advertisements of milliners and mercers; no rich and varied assortment of dress fabrics such as fill the columns of New England and even of Pennsylvania and New York papers of those dates. I fear that southern dames knew few of the pleasures of shopping; they seldom tip-toed on clogs or pattens or rode in sedan chairs through narrow, crowded streets to mantua-makers' and haberdashers' shops, or on board great foreign-laden ships, or on the teeming wharfs alongside, and pulled over the lading of India gauzes and muslins and

Italian silks and Dutch linens, as did favored northern housewives. They prosaically sent long lists to London merchants, who could be paid from the next crop of tobacco, and then waited patiently for return ships to bring to them year-old fashions. One London house had thirty Virginia planters, to whom it sent a yearly supply of apparel. In a few cities—Annapolis and Charleston—great elegance of attire could be seen, but throughout the surrounding counties not nearly as universal modishness as obtained in northern villages and towns. Even runaway servants were far less showily and handsomely dressed; possibly because there were proportionately far more servants and slaves to be dressed.

That many southern women dressed in a graceful and elegant fashion we learn from existing portraits. That of Anne Francis, who married James Tilghman and became the mother of the Revolutionary soldier Colonel Tench Tilghman, displays a lovely countenance, with a dress of much beauty and simplicity. That of the unhappy Evelyn Byrd, of Westover, Va., is equally graceful in dress and carriage. Williamine Wemyss, wife of William Moore, of Moore Hall, Pa., is attired in a more picturesque, almost in grotesque fashion, in sacque and coquettish feathered hat. The wife of Governor Spotswood displays in her portrait a rich and charming garb.

We know very well what a young Virginia miss of gentle birth needed as fashionable and proper attire in 1737—what articles were included in her wardrobe—through the order given by Col. John Lewis for his young ward. It reads thus:

A cap, ruffle, and tucker, the lace 5*s.* per yard.
1 pair White Stays.
8 pair White kid gloves.
2 pair Colour'd kid gloves.
2 pair worsted hose.
3 pair thread hose.
1 pair silk shoes laced.
1 pair morocco shoes.
4 pair plain Spanish shoes.
2 pair calf shoes.
1 Mask.
1 Fan.
1 Necklace.
1 Girdle and Buckle.
1 Piece fashionable Calico.
4 yards Ribbon for knots.

1 Hoop Coat.
1 Hat.
1 1-2 Yard of Cambric.
A Mantua and Coat of Slite Lustring.

A decade later George Washington ordered from England for his little step-daughter—"Miss Custis"—a very full list of costly and modish garments:

8 pairs kid mitts.
4 " gloves.
2 " silk shoes.
4 " Calamanco shoes.
4 " leather pumps.
6 " fine thread stockings.
4 " " worsted "
2 Caps.
2 pairs Ruffles.
2 tuckers, bibs, and aprons if Fashionable.
2 Fans.
2 Masks.
2 bonnets.
1 Cloth Cloak.
1 Stiffened Coat of Fashionable silk made to pack-thread stays.
6 yards Ribbons.
2 Necklaces.
1 Pair Silver Sleeve Buttons with Stones.
6 Pocket Handkerchiefs.

A little girl four years of age, in kid mitts, a mask, a stiffened coat, with pack-thread stays, a tucker, ruffles, bib, apron, necklace, and fan, was indeed a typical example of the fashionable follies of the day.

The step-son — Master Custis — was six years old and was fitted out with equal care:

6 Pocket Handkerchiefs, small and fine.
6 pairs Gloves.
2 Laced Hats.
2 Pieces India Nankeen.
6 pairs fine Thread Stockings.
4 " Coarse " "
6 " Worsted "
4 " strong shoes.
4 " Pumps.
1 Summer suit of clothes to be made of something light and thin.
1 piece black Hair Ribbon.
1 pair handsome Silver shoe & knee buckles.
1 light duffel cloak with Silver Frogs.

As a pendant to this list of children's clothes may be given the description of her own evening dress, recorded by a school-girl of twelve—Anna Green Winslow—in her diary in 1771:

I was dressed in my yellow coat, black bib and apron, black feathers on my head, my paste comb and all my paste, garnet, marquasett and jet pins, together with my silver plume—my locket, rings, black collar round my neck, black mitts and yards of blue ribbon (black and blue is high taste) striped tucker & ruffles (not my best) and my silk pompedore shoes completed my dress.

Other school-girls dressed equally well. The little daughters of General Huntington, of Norwich, Conn., were sent at that same date from Norwich to Boston to be "finished" in Boston schools by Boston teachers. The outfit of one of these boarding-school misses comprised twelve silk gowns, but her chaperon wrote that the young lady must have another gown of a "recently imported rich fabric," which was at once procured in order that Miss Huntington's dress might correspond with her rank and station.

It is easy to form a picture of the dress of the first New England colonists. The inventories of the apparel furnished in London to the male settlers of Salem, Mass., and of Piscataquay, N. H., are still in existence and show to us, with minute exactness, the character and quantity of the garments of these New England settlers. The supply to each individual was liberal and of good quality, but the chief characteristic was durability. Both the breeches and long hose were of leather or of heavy woollens lined with leather. The Salem planters stepped on shore in 1628 in either long hose or breeches. By 1635 the New Hampshire settlers had made a decided advancing step in fashion in this portion of the attire—the long hose were then quite out of date. The doublets and jerkins of both companies of colonists were of leather, the cassocks of cloth or canvas, usually fastened with hooks and eyes —buttons were a vanity. Strong and warm caps and hats were in abundance; also heavy shoes and stockings. The leather and calf-skin garments were, of course, quiet in color, as were the mandillions or cloaks, but the caps were of scarlet, and the waistcoats were also scarlet or of green bound about with red; and in 1633 we find that Governor Winthrop had several dozen scarlet coats sent from England to the Bay. The consigner wrote, "I could not find any Bridgwater cloth but Red; so all the coats sent are red lined with blew, and lace suitable ; which red is the choise color of all.'' So all was not sad-colored and dun in the new land on the shores of the Bay or the banks of the Piscataquay.

The good wives had correspondingly simple, durable, and plentiful attire, appropriate for the laborious life they were forced to lead, and for the rigorous climate they encountered. But by 1650 the plenteous crops, growing industries, and free commercial exchange had, as Johnson noted at that date in his *Wonder Working Providence*, brought comfort and prosperity to Massachusetts—and there also had entered a desire for finer and costlier attire. The durable and appropriate leather doublets and breeches were often replaced by garments of fine wool, and even frail damask and velvet were suggested. The good wives' gowns and cloaks were also shaped from far more costly and more beautiful fabrics. Alarmed and indignant at this veering toward cavalier ways, the watchful Connecticut and Massachusetts magistrates at once passed sumptuary laws to restrain and to attempt to prohibit this luxury and extravagance of dress.

An estate of at least £200 was held necessary in order to allow any freedom of costly or gay attire.

We can be sure that the stern Puritan lawmakers did not base these prohibitory laws on single instances of flaunting finery; so let us see what excess in apparel had become common enough in New England to warrant an alarmed attempt at extirpation. The Massachusetts magistrates prohibited the wearing of gold, silver or thread lace; all cut-works, embroideries, or needlework in the form of caps, bands or rails; gold and silver girdles, hat-bands, belts, ruffs, or beaver hats; knots of ribbon; broad shoulder-bands; silk roses; double ruffles or capes; gold and silver buttons; silk points; silk and tiffany hoods and scarfs. Truly a fine array of follies. No wonder the thrifty souls were alarmed when they beheld such gay and varied bedizenings and bedeckings. And the cut and fashioning of the settlers' garments became extreme. Women displayed immoderate great sleeves and rails; and men walked in immoderate great sleeves and boots and breeches; both wore slashed apparel and long wings—a specially offensive fashion.

Vain offenders against these sumptuary laws were presented by scores, and were tried and fined; and the selectmen of various towns were arraigned for not prosecuting the culprits. And the ministers preached at them, and had tracts printed to warn and deter them; but still the haughty daughters and proud sons "psisted in fflonting" until both preachers and magistrates gave up the unequal struggle in despair, and yielded gloomily with dire memories of Sodom and Gomorrah, and premonitions of similar and speedy annihilation.

The rich wardrobe of Colonel Thomas Richbell, who died in Boston in 1682, must have sorely vexed the stern magistrates, and he must have appeared to them a gay flamboyant peacock in sober Boston streets. His clothing was inventoried thus, and the inventory is now in the Suffolk Probate Court.

	£.	s.	d.
1 Sattin coate wth Gold Flowers & blew breeches, ...	4	0	0

	£.	s.	d.
1 Scarlet coate & breeches wth Silver Buttons, ... 1 P[r] w[ht] Damask breeches, ...	8	0	0
1 Stuffe Suite with Gold Buttons, . .	2	10	
1 Silk Crape Suite,.	1		
1 Stuffe Suite with Silke Buttons, . .	1		
1 Black Cloth Suite, ...	1		
1 Stuffe Suite with Lace, ...	1		
1 haire Chamlett coate wth Froggs, .	2		
7 p[r] white thread hose, 20s. 7 white wastcoats, ...	3	4	
4 p[r] Silke, 1 p[r] Scarlet worsted hose,	2		
12 shirts L8 3 p[r] Holland drawers 12s.,	8	12	
11 handkerchers, 18s. 3 caps, 3s., . .	1	1	
7 Cravats & 7 p[r] Ruffels & Ribbands,	7		
3 hatts & bands, ...	2	10	
2 Rapiers wth Silver hilts & a belt, .	12		
1 Cane wth Silver Head, ...		10	
3 small Periwiggs, ...	3		
1 Diamond Ring & Mourning Ring, .	3		
1 p[r] Bootes, ...		20	

But many simple folk, throughout the seventeenth century, continued to dress plainly, and offered by their frugality and abstinence a foundation on which for a while these sumptuary statutes could be based. Leather breeches, especially, continued to be worn by thrifty townsmen and farm-folk as well as hunters, as long as breeches were worn at all. "Leather breeches-makers" advertise in American newspapers till this century.

Women's attire when simple in material was often varied in shape. Jane Humphrey of Dorchester, Mass., a woman of no wealth, died in 1668. She owned a red kersey, a blemmish serge, a red serge, a black serge, and a green linsey woolsey petticoat—five petticoats in all; a sad grey kersey, a white fustian, a green serge, a blue, and a murry waistcoat—five waistcoats to correspond; two jumps; a blue short coat; a green under coat; a staning kersey coat; a fringed whittle; a cloak; black silk, calico and holland neckcloths; white, blue, holland, and green aprons; quoifes and queues and hoods and muffs; a wardrobe which was certainly sufficient in quantity and which also offered variety.

No better expounder could be found of the style of dress and expense of dress-making and tailoring of a well-to-do New England family in those days, than this tailor's bill of William Sweatland for work done for Jonathan Corwin of Salem. The manuscript of the bill is in the library of the American Antiquarian Society:

	£.	s.	d.
Sept. 29, 1679. To plaiting a gown for M$^{rs.}$		3	6
To makeing a Childs Coat, ...		6	
To makeing a Scarlett petticoat with Silver Lace for M$^{rs.}$		9	
For new makeing a plush somar for M$^{rs.}$		6	
Dec. 22, 1679. For making a somar for your Maide, ...		10	
Mar. 10, 1679. To a yard of Callico, .		2	
To 1 Douzen and ½ of silver buttons, .		1	6
To Thread, ...			4
To makeing a broad cloth hatte, . . .		14	
To making a haire Camcottcoat, . .		9	
To making new halfsleeves to a silk Coascett, ...		1	
March 25. To altering and fitting a paire of Stays for M$^{rs.}$		1	
Ap. 2, 1680, to makeing a Gowne for ye Maide, ...		10	
May 20. For removeing buttons of y^{r} coat, ...			6
Juli 25, 1630. For makeing two Hatts and Jacketts for your two sonnes, .		19	
Aug. 14. To makeing a white Scarsonnett plaited Gowne for M$^{rs.}$ . .		8	
To makeing a black broad cloth Coat for yourselfe, ...		9	

	£.	s.	d.
Sep. 3, 1868. To making a Silke Laced Gowne for Mrs.	1	8	
Oct. 7, 1680, to makeing a Young Childs Coate, ...		4	
To faceing your Owne Coat Sleeves, .		1	
To new plaiting a petty Coat for Mrs. .		1	6
Nov. 7. To makeing a black broad Cloth Gowne for Mrs.		18	
Feb. 26, 1680–1. To Searing a Petty Coat for Mrs.		6	
Sum is,	£8.	4s.	10d.

The dress of the settlers on the Connecticut Valley differed little from that of the Puritans on the coast. Richard Sawyer died in 1648 in Windsor, Connecticut; his wearing apparel was thus inventoried:

	£.	s.	d.
1 musck-colour'd cloth doublitt & breeches, ...	1		
1 bucks leather doublitt, ...		12	
1 calves leather doublitt, ...		6	
1 liver-colour'd doublitt & jacket & breeches, ...		7	
1 haire-colour'd doublitt & jackett & breeches, ...		5	
1 paire canvas drawers, ...		1	6
1 olde coate. 1 paire old gray breeches,		5	

	£.	s.	d.
1 stuff jackett, ...		2	6
1 paire greene knit mens hose, . . .		2	
1 paire old knit cotten hose, . . .		1	6
1 old coloured hatt, ...		3	
1 new coloured hatt, ...		7	
10 Bands, ...		15	
3 shirts, ...		12	
1 paire old boots, ...		5	
1 paire old shoes, ...		2	
1 paire cloth buskins, ...		7	

Goodman Sawyer had a more varied external covering than the Salem settlers, but his undergarments were not equal either in quantity or quality.

The outfit of the Maine colonists was similar, but contained more garments for the use of sailors and fishermen—haling-hands, trushes, slyders, barvells, batts, and broags—as became a fishing community.

At last there arose in New England a truly vain people. From every source open to the antiquary proof can be obtained that, with the early years of the new century, sobriety and economy of dress were lost to the children of the Puritans and Pilgrims. The "pestilent heretics" of Rhode Island, the Quakers, Baptists, and Gortonians, were troubled with no sumptuary legislation, nor were they wealthy enough to be very extravagant; but soon the opulent Narragansett planters could boast a richness of attire that rivalled that of town-folk. In Boston the influence of the Royal Governor and his staff established a miniature court which closely aped English dress and manners, and rivalled English luxury. An English traveller, Bennett, wrote of Boston in 1740, "Both the ladies and gentlemen dress and appear as gay in common as courtiers in England on a coronation or birthday." Whitefield complained bitterly of the "foolish virgins of New England covered all over with the pride of life;" of the jewels, patches, and gay apparel commonly worn. Other travellers made similar observations on the bravery of the modes; and from the account-books and letter-books of merchants, the lists of the wardrobes of deceased persons, the printed advertisements of milliners and mercers, we obtain proof of great luxury and richness of dress, which lasted throughout the century. The attire of the signers of the Declaration of Independence showed no Republican simplicity.

With all this love of dress and the lavish expenditure for rich attire, there came no wastefulness. The papers abound in advertisements of dyers who will new calender and dye old gowns and cloaks and refinish old stuffs and silks. We find even so fine a lady as Peter Faneuil's sister, Mary Ann, sending her gowns to London to be dyed and returned to her; and her old gloves and shoe-roses and shoe-strings to be sold. And clothing was carefully bequeathed by will; sometimes a garment served through three generations.

We have a most interesting and valuable contribution to our knowledge of colonial dress in New York, in the list of the wardrobe of the widow of Dr. Jacob De Lange, of New York, in 1682. It consisted of twelve costly petticoats, six samares, and other articles in smaller number. It was far richer than any list I have ever seen of the possessions of New England goodwives. The jewels are exceptionally rich; I doubt if any woman in New England had such at that time. The silver girdle-chain and embroidered purse were Dutch, not English fashions. The list reads thus:

	£.	s.	d.
One under petticoat with a body of red bay, ...		1	7
One under petticoat, scarlet, ...		1	15
One petticoat, red cloth with black lace, .		2	15
One striped stuff petticoat with black lace, ...		1	8
Two colored drugget petticoats with gray linings, ...		1	2
Two colored drugget petticoats with white linings, ...			18
One colored drugget petticoat with pointed lace, ...			8
One black silk petticoat with ash gray silk lining, ...		1	10
One potto-foo silk petticoat with black silk lining, ...		2	15
One potto-foo silk petticoat with taffeta lining, ...		1	13
One silk potoso-à-samare with lace, . .		3	
One tartanel samare with tucker, ...		1	10
One black silk crape samare with tucker, .		1	10
Three flowered calico samares, ...		2	17
Three calico nightgowns, one flowered, two red, ...			7
One silk waistcoat, one calico waistcoat, .			14
One pair of bodice, ...			4
Five pair white cotton stockings, ...			9

	£.	s.	d.
Three black love-hoods, ...		5	
One white love-hood, ...		2	6
Two pair sleeves with great lace, ...	1	3	
Four cornet caps with lace, ...	3		
One black silk rain cloth cap, ...		10	
One black plush mask, ...		1	6
Four yellow lace drowlas, ...		2	
One embroidered purse with silver bugle and chain to the girdle and silver hook and eye, ...	1	4	
One pair black pendants, gold nocks, . .		10	
One gold boat, wherein thirteen diamonds & one white coral chain, ...	16		
One pair gold stucks or pendants each with ten diamonds, ...	25		
Two diamond rings, ...	24		
One gold ring with clasp beck, ...		12	
One gold ring or hoop bound round with diamonds, ...	2	10	

Dr. De Lange's wardrobe was abundant, but not so rich:

	£.	s.	d.
1 Grosgrained cloak lined with silk, . . .	2	10	
1 Black broadcloth coat, ...	1	10	
1 Black broadcloth suit, ...	1	15	
1 Coat lined with red serge, ...	1	15	
2 Old coats, ...	1	10	
1 Black grosgrained suit, ...	1	14	
1 Coloured cloth waistcoat with silver buttons, ...	1	4	

	£.	s.	d.
1 Coloured serge suit with silver buttons, .	5		
3 silk drawers, ...	2		
2 Calico drawers, ...		2	6
3 White drawers, ...		6	
1 pair yellow hand gloves with black silk fringe, ...		14	
5 pair white Calico Stockings, ...		9	
1 pair Black worsted Stockings, ...		4	
1 pair gray worsted Stockings, ...		5	
1 fine black hat, 1 old gray hat, 1 black hat, ...	1	10	

As no breeches are named in this inventory, and such a goodly number of coats, I think the eight pairs of drawers were summer breeches.

When Cornelius Stienwerck, a wealthy man, Mayor of New York, died at about that same date, he left in one room—his "great chamber"—twelve coats, eight pair breeches, three cloaks and two doublets.

The outfit of the wife of a respectable and well-to-do Dutch settler in New Netherlands differed somewhat from that of Madame De Lange. Vrouentje Ides Stoffelsen left behind her in 1641 a gold hoop ring, a silver medal and chain and a silver undergirdle to hang keys on ; a damask furred jacket, two black camlet jackets, two doublets—one iron gray, the other black ; a blue, a steel-gray lined petticoat, and a black coarse camlet-lined petticoat ; two black skirts, a new bodice, two white waistcoats, one of Harlem stuff ; a little black vest with two sleeves, a pair of damask sleeves, a reddish morning gown, not lined ; four pair pattens, one of Spanish leather ; a purple apron and four blue aprons ; nineteen cambric caps and four linen ones ; a fur cap trimmed with beaver ; nine linen handkerchiefs trimmed with lace, two pair of old stockings, and three shifts. One disposed to be critical might note the somewhat scanty proportion of underclothing in this wardrobe, and as Ides's husband swore "by his manly troth" that the list of her possessions was a true and complete one, we are forced to believe that it was indeed all the underclothing she possessed.

In the following century, many New York women had rich jewels. Mary Duyckinck Sinclair in 1736 bequeathed by will:

One gold chaane of five strings. One neclase of Large Perels. One Large Diamond ring. One gold

Watch. One Picter set in gold. One paer of gold Ear Rings with Learge Perels set in them. One necklase of perels of five strings and gold Lockit. One gold ring with a red stone. One gold Cross laaid in with Pressious stones. One gold Girdel Buckell. One gold hair Neadell.

By Revolutionary times love of dress everywhere prevailed throughout the State of New York—a love of dress which caused great extravagance and was noted by all travellers.

The Chevalier de Crèvecœur gave his testimony to the extravagance of New York fair ones, saying, "If there is a town on the American continent where English luxury displayed its follies it is in New York. . . . In the dress of the women you will see the most brilliant silks, gauzes, hats and borrowed hair." Miss Rebecca Franks, a Philadelphia belle, wrote in 1778 of society in New York:

You can have no idea of the life of continued amusement I live in; I can scarce have a moment to myself. I have stole this while everybody is retired to dress for dinner. I am but just come from under Mr. J. Black's hands, and most elegantly dressed am I for a ball this evening at Smith's, where we have one every Thursday. I wish to Heaven you were going with us this evening to judge for yourself. . . .

The Dress is more ridiculous and pretty than anything I ever saw—great quantity of different colored feathers on the head at a time besides a thousand other things. The Hair dress'd very high, in the shape Miss Vining's was the night we return'd from Smith's—the Hat we found in your Mothers closet wou'd be of a proper size. I have an afternoon cap with one wing, tho' I assure you I go less in the fashion than most of the Ladies—no being dress'd without a hoop. . . . No loss for partners. Even I am engaged to seven different gentlemen, for you must know 'tis a fixed rule never to dance but two dances at a time with the same person. Oh, how I wish Mr. P. wou'd let you come in for a week or two—tell him I'll answer for your being let to return. I know you are as fond of a gay life as myself—you'd have an opportunity of rakeing as much as you choose at either Plays, Balls, Concerts or Assemblys.

A Hessian officer wrote with equal decision of the extravagance of fair country maids, throughout the State:

They are great admirers of cleanliness and keep themselves well shod. They friz their hair every day and gather it up on the back of the head into a chignon at the same time puffing it up in front. They generally walk about with their heads uncovered and sometimes but not often wear some light fabric on their hair. Now and then some country nymph has her hair flowing down behind her, braiding it with a piece of ribbon. Should they go out even though they be living in a hut, they throw a silk wrap about themselves and put on gloves. They also put on some well made and stylish little sunbonnet, from beneath which their roguish eyes have a most fascinating way of meeting yours. In the English colonies the beauties have fallen in love with red silk or woolen wraps. The wives and daughters spend more than their incomes allow. The man must fish up the last penny he has in his pocket. The funniest part of it is the women do not seem to steal it from them, neither do they obtain it by cajoling, fighting, or falling in a faint. How they obtain it is a mystery, but that the men are heavily taxed for their extravagance is certain. The daughters keep up their stylish dressing because their mothers desire it. Nearly all articles necessary for the adornment of the female sex are very scarce and dear. For this reason they are wearing their Sunday finery. Should this begin to show signs of wear I am afraid that the husbands and fathers will be compelled to make peace with the Crown if they would keep their women folk supplied with gewgaws.

The Quakers, through custom and denominational law, were pledged to simple, sober, and uniform dress; yet even they felt the love of dress, which was so strongly crescent everywhere throughout the colonies in the early part of the eighteenth century. In 1726 the "woman ffriends" at the Yearly Meeting at Burlington, felt constrained to send, through their spokeswoman, Hannah Hill, a formal deprecatory message to their fellow women-Quakers. It ran thus:

As first, that Immodest fashion of hooped petticoats or the imitation either by something put into their petticoats to make them set full, or any other imitation whatever, which we take to be but a branch springing from the same corrupt root of pride. And also that none of our ffriends accustom themselves to wear the gowns with superfluous folds behind, but plain and decent, nor go without aprons, nor to wear superfluous gathers or plaits in their caps or pinners, nor to wear their heads drest high behind; neither to cut or lay their hair on their foreheads or temples.

And that ffriends be careful to avoid wearing striped shoes or red and white heeled shoes or clogs, or shoes trimmed with gaudy colors.

And also that no ffriends use that irreverent practice of taking snuff or handing a snuff box one to the other in meeting.

Also that ffriends avoid the unnecessary use of fans in meetings lest it direct the mind from the more inward and spiritual exercises which all ought to be concerned in.

And also that ffriends do not accustom themselves to go with bare breasts or bare necks.

By Benjamin Franklin's day Philadelphians were as fond of dress as were other Americans. Even that rigid and thrifty economist sent home from France, to his Deborah and his daughter, silk negligées, white cloaks and plumes, satin cardinals, and paste shoe-buckles, that they might not "dress with singularity." By Revolutionary days Philadelphia outdid other towns in folly, and surpassed them in lavishness; coming to a climax of astonishing frivolity and extravagance in that extraordinary and picturesque revel, the Meschianza — a pageant more resembling a royal masque than an assembly in a staid Quaker town. General Greene declared the luxury of Boston "an infant babe" to that of Philadelphia. Another officer wrote to General Wayne. "The town is all gayety, and every lady and gentleman endeavors to outdo the other in splendor and show;" and we read in Washington's diary, in Adams's, of the luxury and display in Philadelphia.

It is curious to note that the succession of events in European and American history can be traced through the commemorative names given to garments worn in colonial days. Ramillies and Campaign wigs, Quebec cloaks, Garrick hats, Brunswick cloaks, Kitty Fisher bonnets, all show the marks of passing events or historic or notorious personages. At a later date, when French ideas so largely dominated in America, French names and references constantly appear; a notable example being the various applications of the words air-balloon and parachute at the beginning of the aëronautic craze. The opening of the East India trade brought to America many Chinese and Indian stuffs, the names of which are now nearly all obsolete. I have given in my book, *Customs and Fashions in Old New England*, over one hundred names of oriental stuffs, whose exact definition cannot now be indicated, and which were of silk, cotton, linen, or cotton and silk, and were usually gauzes, cottons, or muslins for summer wear, which took their name from the Indian town or community where they were manufactured.

I have also noted in the same book the curious fact that, from the letters and diaries of early days, we gain a notion not so much of the vanity of our grandmothers as of our grandfathers. Comparatively few letters written by colonial women have been preserved; indeed, the women of those days were not great letter-writers, and their rare letters seldom refer to dress. But the letters of their husbands and brothers speak with no uncertain voice of the pains these good, sober, pious gentlemen took with their garments—their satisfaction in becoming clothing; their intense discontent over ill-fitting or ill-colored attire. They are as eager for "patterns" and modes as any country girl on her first visit to town. Here is a portion of a letter written to New London in June, 1706, by John Winthrop, a young Boston spark, to a fellow-dandy, his uncle Fitz-John Winthrop, a sedately foppish old gentleman of nearly seventy summers:

> Since my last I have picked up at severall shopps in towne a parcell of patternes which are inclosed. There is no choise of anything. Everything very ordinary and extravigantly dear. It was an accidentall thing I litt upon y[t] camblett which was very good and very cheap as times goe. As soon as ever I see it at Banisters shopp I thought it was ye genteelest thing I had seen anywhere.

Yo^{r} Honours Cote, my Cote, Govr Dudleys cote and his sonns cote took up ye whole piece. There is no cloths y^{t} are fitt for a jackett and britches for yor Honour & if there were they would be too hott for summer; and no silks but a parcell of slimsey gaudy things that yor Honour would not like. It is a great fashion here to wear West India linnens. I have enclos'd some of ye best patternes. They make pretty light cool wastcotes and britches. Everybody of any fashion wears them in summer.

Scores of reference to dress abound in the letters of Wait Winthrop, that solid man of Boston, and of his brother Fitz-John. Very rarely women's attire is ordered, and with but scant explanation, simply a gown or a petticoat; but for their own masculine garments such sentences as these were exchanged by the brothers:

I desire you to bring me a very good camlet cloake lyned with what you like except blew. It may be purple or red or striped with those or other colors if so worn suitable and fashionable. . . . I would make a hard shift rather than not have the cloak.

I have sent youre sute by Major Palmer. The stufe was ye most fashionable y^{t} could be got. Y^{t} which is most in weare is a drugett but here is not a piece in town.

I have endeavour'd to sute you with what you wrote for; the coate is of the best drab de bury in towne. The serge as fine as I could get.

Indeed, John Winthrop ordered so many suits in Boston that I did not wonder at his brother-in-law's suggestion that he wear out those he already had ere he bought others. Even petty articles, such as hats and shoes, received from him vast attention, and he condescended much to buttons and made careful drawings and descriptions of modish buttonholes which he desired. A certain buckled buff belt caused so much exchange of correspondence that it was truly a Girdle of Opakka, a symbol of prudence, thrift, and decision.

Rough old Governor Belcher was equally fond of dress. In 1740 he wrote thus to his son:

In this bundle is a leathern wastcoat & breeches which get lac'd with gold in the handsomest manner; not open or bone lace but close lace something open near the head of the lace. Let it be substantial strong lace. The buttons to be metal buttons with eyes of the same, not buttons with wooden molds & catgut loops which are good for nothing. They must be gilt with gold & wrought in imitations of buttons made with thread or wire. You must also send me a fine cloth jockey coat of same colour with the wastcoat and breeches, and lined with a fine shalloon of same colour, & trim'd plain, onely a button with same sort as that of the wastcoat but proportionably bigger. The coat may be made to fit me by the wastcoat. I must also have two pair of fine worsted hose to match this suit, and a very good hatt laced or not as may be the fashion, and a sett of silver buckles for shoes & knees & another sett of pinchbeck. . . . I desire to buy me as much three pile black velvet such as is made for mens wear and the best can be had for money, as much as will make me a compleat suit, the buttons and holes to be of the same with the cloaths, and the lining of the best double shagrine of a dark gold colour, if that not to be had some other good lining silk of that colour. I herewith deliver you my measure that the cloaths may be made to, and rather too big than too little. I desire you also to buy me a nightgown of the best Genoa damask that is made for mens wear. Let the gown be every way large enough for you and it will fitt me. Let the colour of the outside and lining be a deep crimson. And I would have to spare a yard of the velvet & two of the damask.

Though he characterized himself as "a poor Governor living from hand to mouth," these letters of Belcher's indicate no poverty, and his portrait displays a rich embroidered coat and waistcoat with fine laces and elaborate frogs and buttons.

From the days of his early manhood George Washington showed a truly proper—indeed, I may say a truly masculine love of dress. We find him in 1747, when a lad of fifteen, making this careful note for a tailor:

> Memorandum. To have my coat made by the following Directions, to be made a Frock with a Lapel Breast. The Lapel to contain on each side six Button Holes & to be about 5 or 6 inches wide all the way equal, & to turn as the Breast on the Coat does, to have it made very long Waisted and in Length to come down to or below the bent of the knee, the Waist from the Armpit to the Fold to be exactly as long or Longer than from thence to the Bottom, not to have more than one fold in the Skirt and the top to be made just to turn in and three Button Holes, the Lapel at the top to turn as the Cape of the Coat and Button to come parallel with the Button Holes and the Last Button Hole on the Breast to be right opposite the Button on the Hip.

After his marriage to a rich widow, Washington showed equal interest in the dress of his increased family. In one order in 1759, he sent for these articles of wearing apparel for himself and his wife; and as he said, "particularized the sorts, qualities, and taste, all to be good and fashionable of their several kinds."

A Light Summer Suit made of Duroy by the measure.
4 pieces Best India Nankeen.
2 best plain beaver Hats at 21*s*.
1 piece Black Satin Ribbon.
1 Sword belt red morocco or buff, no buckles or rings.
A Salmon Coloured Tabby of the Enclosed Pattern to be made in a sack & coat.
A Cap, Handkerchief, Tucker, & Ruffles to be made of Brussels Lace or point proper to be worn with the above negligee, to cost £20.
2 Fine Flowered Aprons.
1 pair womans white silk hose.
6 " " fine cotton "
4 " " " thread "
1 pair black satin, 1 pair white satin shoes of smallest 5s.
4 " calamanco shoes.
1 Fashionable hat or bonnet.
6 pairs Womens best Kid Gloves.
8 " " " " Mitts.
1-2 Dozen Knots & Breastknots.
1 " Round Silk Laces.
1 Black Mask.
1 Dozen most Fashionable Cambric Pockethandkerchiefs.

Washington throughout his life never let affairs of state or war crowd out his love of fitting and rich attire ; and in every order to England, the instructions to secure the latest modes, the reigning fashion, were strenuously dwelt upon. Other Revolutionary heroes were equally vain, and vied with judges, doctors, and merchants, in rich and carefully studied attire ; but Washington was

> The expectancy and rose of the fair state,
> The glass of fashion, and the mould of form,
> The observed of all observers.

Costume of Colonial Times

COSTUME OF COLONIAL TIMES

ALAMODE. A plain soft glossy silk much like lustring or our modern surah silk, but more loosely woven. It was originally made on the Continent, and is said to have been first made in England in 1693 in the reign of William and Mary. I find from Judge Sewall's letter-book, published by the Massachusetts Historical Society, that he ordered it, with other dress fabrics, from England as early as 1687. In 1697 John Lane, of Woburn, Mass., left "20 els of alamod" by will. The name appears constantly until after Revolutionary times, certainly until 1785, in New England and Southern newspapers, in milliners', mercers', and other shopkeepers' lists, under the various and ingenious spellings with which our forbears managed to vary their orthography—elamond, alimod, olamod, alemod, arlimod, allamode, and ellimod—and must have been widely used. In the *Boston News Letter* of September 15, 1715, is an early advertisement which reads, "Allamods French and English." I also find allamode fringes advertised in the *Boston Evening Post* of June, 1756. It was largely employed for mantuas and hoods and for linings for rich garments.

ALLAPINE. This woollen stuff, also spelled ellapine, allpine, alpine, was frequently mentioned in public and private inventories of the first half of the eighteenth century. It must have been strong and good, for it was not cheap. It was apparently used exclusively for men's wear. Captain William Templer's best suit of garments was a "double Allpine coat and breeches" and was worth £25. In 1741 William Bennet's "Speckled Jacket and Breeches" of allapine were worth £9. Allapine was advertised in the *Boston News Letter* in 1739 and 1742, but I have not found it named in newspapers of later dates.

APRON.

These aprons white of finest thrid,
  So choicely tide, so dearly bought,
So finely fringed, so nicely spred,
  So quaintlie cut, so richlie wrought.

— *Pleasant Quippes for New-Fangled UpStart Gentlewomen. 1596.*

I doubt not many an apron came over in the Mayflower. Wood in his *New England's Prospects*, 1634, speaks of ordering "Green Sayes for aprons." Early inventories of the effects of emigrant dames contain many an item of those housewifely garments: Jane Humphreys, of Dorchester, Mass., had in her good wardrobe, in 1668, "2 Blew aprons, A White Holland Apron with a Small Lace at the bottom. A White Holland Apron with two breathes in it. My best white apron. My greene apron." After the death of Madam Usher, who had been the widow of President Leonard Hoar of Harvard College, and who had a rich wardrobe, much of her clothing was sent to her daughter, in 1725; among the items enumerated were, "9 aprons, five of them short." By this time aprons had become an indisputable, almost an essential part of a fine lady's attire. Queen Anne wore them, and of course all fashionable and loyal women in England did likewise and in New England also. As soon as advertisements of dress goods and articles of dress appeared in New England newspapers, such notices as this were found—of the *New England Weekly Journal* of 1739, "Beautiful Gold and Silver Brocade Aprons;" of 1740, "Short Aprons wrought with Gold," "Minuet Aprons;" or this of Sally Trippers of Draw Lane, Hartford, in 1766, "Female Aprons for ladies from eighteen to fifty." Striped gauze and "drest picket" and lawn-embroidered aprons appear, showing that they were purely an ornamental, not a useful adjunct to the toilet. Lessons were given and patterns sold for embroidering aprons, in Dresden work, cross-stitch, and darned work. Sample aprons were sent from England and eagerly copied by deft-fingered New England dames. Until well into this century aprons were worn—indeed until our own day, when the pretty feminine fancy has been too much given over to servant maids.

ARLIMOD. See Alamode.

ARMOZINE. Also ARMOISINE and ARMAZINE. A strong corded silk used from the time of Elizabeth to that of George III. In *Hakluyt's Voyages* we read of "armesine of Portugall." I presume the "Black Ermozeen" advertised in the *Massachusetts Gazette* of September 26, 1771, was armozine. I have also found it in inventories spelled armazine. It was used for gowns for women and waistcoats for men.

ARTOIS. A long cloak made with several capes and worn by women about 1790. It had lapels and revers like a box-coat.

BAIZE. This was quite as frequently spelt bayes. It was a coarse woollen cloth made at Norwich and Colchester in the time of Elizabeth, and called Colchester baize as late certainly as 1775, for in the *Connecticut Courant* of December 11 of that year, "common blue and white Colchester baize" was advertised for sale, and "white bayes" also. In Peter Faneuil's time—1737—it was worth five shillings a yard. We often find it composing portions of the dress of runaway servants, especially the petticoats and jackets of negro slaves.

BAND. A stiff collar of linen or cambric worn by nearly all Puritans. We read in the *Character of a Roundhead*, 1640:

What creature's this with his short hairs,
His little band, and huge long ears,
That this new faith hath founded?

Four plain and three falling bands were supplied to each settler of Massachusetts Bay. The various shapes may be seen in the portraits of the times. They were usually severely simple—indeed, embroidered and broad bands were forbidden by sumptuary laws in New England. They were sometimes fastened by narrow ferret or by band-strings, cords, and tassels, as in the portrait of Governor Winslow (1645), and of Governor Endicott (1655). Geneva bands were worn by the ministers. Women wore laced bands. Lawyer Lechford in his note-book gave the cost of eighteen bands as thirty-six shillings, in 1639. The judges of the Supreme Court wore bands when on the bench till this century. See Falling-Band.

BANDILIER. A case of wood or metal covered with leather and strung with cord on a belt. The cover was made to slip up and down on the cord that it might not be lost. It contained charges of powder, and thus formed part of a soldier's outfit. The band holding these bandiliers was frequently of strong neat's leather, and was sometimes worn over one shoulder and hung down under the opposite arm. In certain accounts of the times the word bandileer appears to be applied collectively to the band with its suspended cases, instead of to the case alone.

BANYAN. "A morning gown such as is worn by the Banians." In 1735 the *New England Weekly Journal* contained an advertisement of "Starretts for Gowns and Banyans," and in 1739 "Scarlet Cloth for Banyans;" in the preceding year the *Weekly Rehearsal* had one of "Banjans made of Worsted Damask Brocaded Stuffs, Scotch Plods and Calliminco." The *Boston News Letter* of 1742, had "Masqueraded

Stuffs suitable for Gown, and Banyans." In the *Boston Gazette* of April 17, 1769, we read of a "Ran away Negro Boy named Robin of yellow complexion and hair, carried off a green flower'd Russell Banyan." A diary of the times speaks in the year 1744 of an Indian child "neatly dressed in a green banjan;" and the will of Colonel Robert Vassall of Cambridge, Mass., left a "Banjan" to his son. So it was evidently a garment like a dressing-gown, made of highly colored or figured cloth and worn by old and young of both sexes; perhaps it is a banyan that appears garishly enveloping the masculine form in many of Copley's portraits — for instance, the one of Nicholas Boylston, in Harvard Memorial Hall. In Virginia these banyans were much worn, so said Wm. Byrd, and were sometimes lined with a rich material, and thus could be worn either side out.

Barlicorns. "Check'd barlicorns" were advertised among dress fabrics in the *Boston Gazette* in 1755, and until Revolutionary times.

Barragons. "Barragons of various figures and colours" were advertised in the *Boston Evening Post* in 1761 and in 1783. The word is also written barraken, barracan, and barragan. Gilbert White described it in his *Selborne* as "a genteel corded stuff much in vogue for summer wear." It was made originally at the Levant, of camel's hair.

Barratine. An obsolete stuff, of which even the description is wholly lost. In the *London Gazette* of 1689, a barratine mantua and petticoat were advertised. In the will of one C. Taylor, of Philadelphia, in 1697, were named a "baratine body, stomacher, petticoat and forehead clothes." I think it was a silk stuff.

Barry. I have read several times of barry-colored gowns. I know of no such color. The heraldic term barry means horizontally barred. A barry gown may have been what we now term bayadère striped.

Barvell. A coarse leathern apron used by workmen, chiefly by fishermen. It is possibly a corruption of *barm*, meaning lap, and *fell*, meaning skin. The name appears in inventories of goods sent by the English Company to America in the seventeenth century, especially to the Maine settlers who were with John Wynter at Richmond's Island, in the years from 1635 to 1640. These inventories are published in the Collections of the Maine Historical Society for the year 1884. We there read of "calue skins for barvells," and find that three barvells were worth nine shillings. By a curious survival, this old English provincial word still may be heard used by the fishermen on the coast of Maine, as well as by English sailors and seamen.

Batts. In the inventories of goods ordered by and sent to John Wynter in 1636, from the English Company, appear frequently such items as "Four Paire Batts." Batts were heavy low shoes, laced in front. The word is still used in Somersetshire for similar shoes.

Bayes. See Baize.

Beads. Beads were a staple article of importation to the new land even in earliest days, being of especial value in trading with the Indians, who coveted them above everything save strong waters. The red men made beads for themselves "work'd out of certain shells so cunningly that neither Jew nor devil could counterfeit." Josselyn, in his *New England's Rarities*, thus described the adornments of the "tawny lasses."

> They are girt about the middle with a Zone wrought with Blue and White Beads into pretty Works. Of these Beads they have Bracelets for the Neck and Arms, and Links to hang in their Ears, and a Fair Table curiously made up with Beads likewise to wear before their Breast. Their Hair they Combe backward and tye it up short with a Border about two Handsfull broad, wrought in works as the other with their Beads.

By newspaper times we read of beads which were intended for the wear of Caucasian dames and maids.

"Sollitaire & Common Black & White Beeds" were offered for sale in the Boston Gazette in 1749. Gold, silver, jet, pearl and marquasite beads also were sold. See BUGLE.

Bearer. A roll or padding placed like a bustle at either hip to raise the skirt. Swift speaks of the "bolsters that supply her hips." We read of a colonial dame "with a coat raised by great bearers."

Beaver. See Hat.

Bedcoat. See Rail.

Beryllian. In the *Pennsylvania Gazette* of 1729, and in the *Charleston Gazette* of 1744, appears frequently this word, in such advertisements as this "Beryllian and other Eastern India Goods for Women's apparell." I do not find the word in any dictionary.

Biggin. A coif worn formerly by men; it came quickly to mean exclusively a child's close cap or hood. Shakespeare speaks of "homely biggins," and they were evidently a cap for everyday wear. The word is probably derived from *béguine*, a nun. The word biggonet was a later derivative and was applied to a woman's cap. We find in the Winthrop Papers Mistress Mary Dudley writing in 1636 to Madame Winthrop for "fine holland for bigins" for her new-born baby. In a masque given at Whitehall in 1639, a chorus of children wore as stage dress "bibs, biggins and muckinders."

BIRDET. "Stript & plain Birdet" were named in the *New England Weekly Journal* in 1737, and "Very nice stript Damsacus and Chinese Burdet for Waistcoats" in 1767. It was apparently an India silk stuff.

BODICE. This article of wear, usually spelt boddice, occasionally appears. More frequently in seventeenth century inventories is seen this form—"a pair of bodyes." These "bodyes" were a bodice in two pieces for outside wear, laced front and back and thus were literally a pair. I think the term was also used for stays.

BODKIN. Originally a dagger, then a "hair-peg" or hair-pin. In the *Triumphant Widow*, 1677, we read:

> Silver bodkins for your hair,
> Bobs which maidens love to wear.

Martha Emmons, of Boston, left in 1666 a "Silver Bodkine," while Widow Susannah Oxenbridge of the same town had, in 1695, a gold bodkin. A silver hair-peg named in 1748 was a hair bodkin. A "hair neadell" was also an ornamental hair-pin—the good old Saxon word *haernaedl.* See HAIRPIN.

BOMBAZIN. A mixture of silk and cotton introduced in the reign of Queen Elizabeth. In 1675 "the Dutch elders presented at court (at Norwich) a specimen of a novel work called bombazines for the manufacturing of which elegant stuff this city has ever since been famed." The name frequently appears in early colonial inventories; "bomber-zeen" was advertised in the *New England Weekly Journal* in 1741, and the stuff has been in wear till our own day.

BONE-LACE. See LACE.

BONNET. The first use that I have chanced to see in New England records of the word bonnet for women's headgear, was in the year 1725, when Madam Usher's wardrobe was sent to England. "Two silk bonnets" were on the list. In the *Boston News Letter* in 1743 it was stated where ladies might have bonnets made, so they must then have become widely worn. In 1760 in the *Boston Evening Post* "Sattin Bonnets" were advertised, and "Quilted Bonnets and Kitty Fisher Bonnets;" and Anna Adams, a Boston milliner, had "Quebeck and Garrick Bonnets." The following year came "Prussian and Ranelagh Bonnets." In July, 1764, came seasonable Leghorn and Queens Bonnets, and then "drawn lace and rich lac'd bonnets," and "women's neat-made mourning bonnets." In Hartford in 1775, Mary Gabiel, "Milliner from France," charged two shillings and six-pence for making newest-fashioned bonnets in the neatest manner, and but a shilling for making a plain bonnet. We gain some notion of the colors fashionably worn, and sold opposite the Liberty Tree. "Plain and Masqueraded newest fashion crimson, blue, pink, white and black bonnets." There is no hint of the shapes of these early bonnets, whether poke or cottage, tunnel or saucer-shaped.

From the portraits of the times I judge the modish head covering for many years to be hats and hoods.

Boots. By the provincial government of Massachusetts it was ordered, in 1651, that no man worth under £200 should be allowed to "walk in great boots." Jonas Fairbanks and Robert Edwards were tried in the Bay Colony for this offence against the commonwealth. As the boots of that day were frequently made cavalier-fashion, with broad, flaring tops, there is no doubt that this law was a frugal measure to discountenance the waste of leather.

In 1641 in the inventory of Edward Skinner, a leather worker, appeared "White Russett Boots;" he also had "5 payr Boots"—made doubtless for wealthy colonists. Advertisements of boots are not plentiful in the early newspapers, though the law about boot-wearing had long ere their day become a dead letter. In 1715, in the *Boston News Letter* appear notices of "English boots, half-jack and small, tops & spurs," and a "fresh hogshead of Half Jack English

Jockey Boots." And at rare intervals jack-boots are advertised until Revolutionary times, but apparently were only for wear on horseback. Top-boots, the delight of bucks and bloods, appeared in the latter half of the century; and with the snowy tops and polished legs formed an elegant foot-gear that deserved its popularity.

Boot-Breeches. See Breechès.

Boot-Hose. These were the same as spatterdashes, q. v. The name and article were in constant use in the Southern colonies. The earliest record is in the will of Zachary Molleshead, of St. Marys, Maryland, in 1638. "Boot-hose tops" also are named.

Bosom Bottle. I was much puzzled by the advertisement in the *Boston Evening Post* of July 26, 1756, and in subsequent newspapers, of "Bosom Bottles." I now believe them to be the small, flat glasses, which, filled with water, were worn in the stomacher of the dress, and in which the stems of "bosom flowers" were placed. No lady at that time was considered to be in full dress unless she wore a bunch of natural flowers in her dress. A bosom bottle, four inches in height, used in the year 1770, was pear-shaped, of heavy ribbed glass. They were sometimes covered with silk the color of the gown, for the purpose of more effectual concealment.

BRACELET. I fancy these pieces of jewelry were rare in America in early days. Ann Clark had a "braselett" in Boston, in 1666, and wealthy Jane Oxenbridge had a carnelian bracelet in 1673; but I do not find any advertisements of them in eighteenth century newspapers, nor do I recall many portraits of that date in which the fair sitters displayed bracelets.

BRASSELETS. "Figur'd & Spangl'd Brasselets" were named among dress-fabrics in the *Boston Evening Post* in November, 1767, and for a decade of years later.

BRAWLS. A blue and white striped cotton cloth made in India. I find it advertised from 1785 to 1795 among other Indian stuffs. It was also spelt brauls.

Breast Knots. We read in the *Weekly Rehearsal* of January 10, 1732, that "in breast knots may be shown a good deal of ingenuity in delicate Choice of Colours & Dispositions; a beautiful Purple is the general Mode." In 1798, in the *Farmers' Weekly*, "the brick dust hue of coquelicot ribands" was said to be the prevailing color in knots. The Federal breast-knot, or rose, was made of black ribbon with a white button or fastening. Bosom-knots were breast-knots.

Breeches. This word was in use as early as the year 1382 when Wiclif wrote of Adam and Eve that they made "briches" of fig-leaves. In still earlier days the Saxons and other breeched barbarians wore the garment.

Though the Bay colonists had "doublet and hose," they also had coats and bryks, or breeches; and they quickly taught the Indians to wear the latter also. This donning of small clothes by the savages was not wholly approved by the colonists, though it is difficult to conjecture the ground of objection. Roger Williams wrote, "I have long had scruples of selling the natives aught but what may tend to bring to civilizing. I therefore neither bought nor shall sell them loose coats nor breeches." King Philip wrote from Mount Hope in 1672, to Colonel Hopestill Foster, of Dorchester, asking for "A pr of good Indian briches and silke & Buttons & 7 yards Gallownes for trimming." We hear of another pair of Indian breeches at Warwick, R. I., in 1656, worth 7*s*. 6*d*. And, indeed, by 1746 so prevalent had English fashions become among American savages that a runaway Indian *maid-servant* was advertised as wearing off "smoked leather breaches."

Breeches-making became a trade in itself, aside from tailoring, because the breeches were commonly made of leather, deer-skin or sheep-skin, and required different workmen. "Philadelphia breeches" of deer-skin cost but $4 a pair. In 1740 we read of "breeches with neither strings nor knee-straps," and again of a runaway "with white knee-strings," and another with "silk knee-straps." Knit breeches came in in 1768 "as low as four pistareens a pair," and "breeches pieces" or "breeches patterns" of velvet, plush, silk, brocade, and other stuffs were sold. The breeches worn by the early planters were fulled at the waist and knee, after the Dutch fashion, somewhat like our modern knickerbockers, or the English bag-breeches. By the latter part of the eighteenth century they were worn skin-tight. A gentleman when ordering a pair is said to have told his tailor, "If I can get into 'em, I won't pay for 'em." A curious item on many inventories of goods sent to John Wynter in Maine, about the year 1640 is "boot-breeches," and we read often of his selling "2 yards Cape Cloth to make a paire boote-breeches." These were gathered full below the knee with a strap.

BROCADE. In the *New England Weekly Journal* of September 29, 1737, we read of a "New parcel fine Brocaded Silks with White Grounds, beautifully Flower'd with Lively Colours." At other dates appear "rich Armozed Ground Brocades," "Flower'd Brocade of Blue Ground" and "Pinck colour Brocade." Tbe brocades of colonial days were exceedingly rich in texture and color; and examples preserved to our own day prove them unrivaled by the products of our modern looms.

Brogue. A heavy coarse shoe made of rawhide, and originally of a single upper piece of untanned leather sewed on a heavy sole, and with a single tie lace. In the inventories of goods consigned to John Wynter in Maine, in 1640, appear "46 paire Brogues," and again "2 paire broags," and "3 paire Irish broags." Nineteen pair of "broags" were worth £1. 8*s.* 10*d.* These were the "clouted brogues" of Shakespeare's day. The Irish word brogan has much the same meaning. In the plural brogues sometimes meant trousers. Washington Irving used the word in that sense.

Brooch. Though doubtless brooches were worn in America in early days, I have not chanced to find them named till 1775, when "mocus and marquasite broaches" were offered for sale. A little later came "gold broaches with devices of hair and pearl."

BRUNSWICK. A habit or riding coat for ladies' wear, said to have been introduced in England in 1750 from Germany. It had collar, lappets and buttons like a man's coat, and of course Boston dames had to follow English fashions; so Boston milliners had Brunswicks for sale, and also Prussian cloaks.

BRYKS. See BREECHES.

BUCKLES. Weeden, in his *Economic and Social History of New England*, says that shoebuckles for women's wear were out of fashion in 1727; but we find that man of importance in the commonwealth—Judge Sewall—giving the Widow Denison, in 1728, a pair that cost five shillings and sixpence. By 1750 we find advertised, in the *Boston Gazette*, "women's white shoebuckles." They must have been in constant wear by men at that date, for they appear in every shopkeeper's list both North and South, and in many of the inventories of goods ordered abroad for children's and grown persons' wear. In the *Connecticut Courant* of May 1, 1773, we read of "silver, plated, and pinchbeck shoe, knee, and stock buckles;" also "bootbuckles and Ladies' Elegant Set Shoe Buckles." Kneebuckles were also an important article of dress, being made of gold and silver and set with paste jewels. Governor Belcher had gold kneebuckles.

BUFFONTS. A full projecting covering for a lady's throat and breast, made of gauze or lace or linen, and much worn from 1750 to 1790, according to English magazines of these years. It was confined by the bodice and puffed out above like the breast of a pouter pigeon. In 1784, in the Salem newspapers, "Thread and Net Buffonts" and "Gauze Buffons" were advertised, and in the *Massachusetts Gazette* of May, 1771, "Hair bouffes and mops."

BUGLES. These tube-shaped black glass beads were offered for sale in Boston as early as 1740, and spelled beaugles. Spenser, in the *Shepherd's Calendar*, 1579, spelt it beaugles.

BUSKINS. In a few inventories I find buskins named. Richard Sawyer, of Windsor,

Conn., had a pair of cloth "buskens" in 1648. As late as 1743 a Boston runaway wore off "gray stockings with blue buskins over them," and a Pennsylvania redemptioner wore sliders with buskins. Buskins were also called kit-packs. They were a sort of half-boot.

BUTTONS. The waistcoats and mandillions and doublets of the Bay colonists were fastened with hooks and eyes, but buttons must have been worn also, for John Eliot ordered for traffic with the Indians in 1651 three gross of pewter buttons. Robert Keayne, of Boston, writing in 1653, said bitterly that a "haynous offence" of his had been selling buttons at too large profit—that they were gold buttons and he had sold them for two shillings ninepence a dozen in Boston, when they had cost but two shillings a dozen in London; which does not seem, in the light of our modern duties on imported goods, a very "haynous" profit. He also added with acerbity that "they were never payd for by those that complayned." These gilt and silvered buttons must have been fashionable, for I find them often named. In a tailor's bill of 1679 I find an item of "1 Dozen & ½ Silver Buttons, 1sh 6d."

Sir William Pepperell, writing to London in 1737, ordered "mohere buttons and mohere answerable," showing that buttons were made to match stuffs; and he also ordered "12 grose Cheap mettal bottens and 12 grose coat bottens." The buttons displayed in his portrait are very large. He did not need to send to London for them; there were for sale at that time in Boston "Gold and Silver Frosted Buttons, Cloth colored Horsehair Buttons All Sorts, Silver Washed Metal Buttons," and many other varieties.

Buttons were made of coins, often of Spanish dollars; and pewter buttons were cast at home in button moulds. A very grotesque form of buttons was of horses' teeth set in brass. By Revolutionary times basket and deathshead buttons became so fashionable and so largely sold that for many years every newspaper throughout the country contained advertisements of them. It is safe to believe that buttons were worn constantly on men's clothes, from the earliest colonial days, and varied but slightly in their position on garments from that of the present day. They were also worn on looped or cocked hats.

Button - Holes. Button - holes were a matter of ornament as well as of use. They were carefully cut and "laid around" bound in gay colors, embroidered, with silver and gold thread, bound with vellum. We find in old-time letters directions about modish button - holes, and drawings even, in order that the shape may be exactly as wished. In the *New England Weekly Journal,* in 1737, we find advertised "Silver and Gold Thread for Button Holes, and Silver and Gold Sleazy Thread for Stitching and embroidering."

Caddis. A woollen tape or coarse crewell used as a cheap trimming or woven into garters. It is frequently spelled cadiss, as in the *Boston News Letter* in 1736, or caddas, caddice and caddes, and often classed with qualities, another coarse binding tape. The word is familiar to us through its use in the works of the old English dramatists. Caddis was in the pedler's pack in *The Winter's Tale*.

Calash.

Hail, great Calash! o'erwhelming veil,
 By all-indulgent Heaven
To sallow nymphs and maidens stale,
 In sportive kindness given.

Thus wrote a Yankee poet in *Rivington's New York Gazette* and in a Norwich newspaper in 1780.

The calash is said to have been invented by the Duchess of Bedford in the year 1765, though similar head-coverings may be seen on English effigies of the sixteenth century. It was an enormous head-covering, a veritable sunshade, which could scarcely be called a bonnet. It was usually made of thin green silk shirred on strong lengths of rattan or whalebone placed two or three inches apart, which were drawn in at the neck; and it was sometimes, though seldom, finished with a narrow cape. It was extendible over the face like the top or hood of an old-fashioned chaise or calash, from which latter it doubtless received its name. It could be drawn out by narrow ribbons or bridles which were fastened to the edge at the top. The calash could also be pushed into a close gathered mass at the back of the head. Thus, standing well up from the head, they formed a good covering for the high-dressed and powdered heads of the date when they fashionably were worn—from 1765 throughout the century; and for the caps worn in the beginning of this century. They were frequently a foot and a half in diameter and were sometimes of brown or gray silk, and I know of two made of thin white dimity, to be worn to evening parties by two young misses about sixty years ago. They were seen on the heads of old ladies in country towns in New England certainly until 1840, and possibly later. In England they were also worn until that date, as we learn from Mrs. Gaskell's *Cranford*, and Thackeray's *Vanity Fair*.

CALICO. Calicoes are spoken of by Josselyn in his *New England's Rarities*, who says that "callicoes and aligers" were readily vendible in New England, and specially sends for "blew-callicoe." John Wynter had six "Calcue Shurtes" in 1636. Pepys wrote forty years later that the English customs officers taxed it as linen, while the East India Company asserted that it was made of cotton wool that grew on trees. Though the name occasionally appears in American inventories and descriptions of the early part of the eighteenth century (as in the possessions of witch Anne Hibbins in 1656, "5 painted Callico curtains & valiants"), calicoes were neither universally nor fashionably worn until after the Revolution, when Brissot wrote: "Calicoes and chintzes dress the women and children." I read in an old newspaper: "Since the peace, calico has become the general fashion of our countrywomen, and is worn by females of all conditions at all seasons of the year, both in town and country." The French calicoes were extremely delicate in color, fine of texture, and high in price, and were worn in midwinter, even in the icy churches. They were also used to trim other and richer materials. Such advertisements as this, from the *Boston Evening Post* in 1743, may frequently be seen: "Demy Chinted Callico Borders for Womens Petticoats."

These calicoes came in many fanciful designs. We read of patterns called "liberty peak," "basket work," "Covent Garden cross-bar," "Ranelagh half-moon," "Prussian stormont," "harlequin moth," "a fine check inclosing four Lions Rampant and three flours de Luce." I have seen old calicoes stamped with portraits of Benjamin Franklin and George Washington, and another design with the presentment of some British officer. As these designs were stamped with blocks by hand, it was easy to order special patterns for special uses, such as bed-hangings. At Deerfield Memorial Hall may be seen a full stock of all the old-time tools and machines used in weaving and printing calico, including the old hand-stamps.

CALLIMANCO. Fairholt says, erroneously, that this was a glazed linen stuff; it was a substantial and fashionable woollen stuff.

The name is said to have meant, originally, a head-covering made of camel's hair; later, by derivation, a vestment of the Pope. It was a woollen stuff of fine gloss, either ribbed or plain, and was used for many articles of men's and women's attire, and largely used in the middle of the last century for women's shoes. It was worn certainly as early as 1666 in America; Martha Emmons, of Boston, left by will at that date a "callimanco gound." In 1592 it had been woven in England. James Fontaine, a Huguenot settler of Virginia, gives in his memoirs a careful account of his attempt to manufacture callimanco in 1694, and says it was made of an extremely fine double twisted worsted thread. Pepperell, writing abroad in 1737, ordered a "peace of flowered Callimanco suitable to make my mother a Wint[r] gown," and the same for his wife. In a letter published in the Collections of the Lexington Historical Society relating to the visit of Washington to that town in November, 1789, we read that, to do him full honor, "Lucindy, pert minx, had a most lovely Gown of Green Callamanco with Plumes to her hatt."

CAMLET. A stuff either of hair, of silk, or of wool, or of all these materials in various combinations, in universal use from early colonial days, especially for cloaks and petticoats. Camlets were also plain, twilled, or of double or single warp, and they frequently were watered. In 1652 Dorothie King, of Weymouth, had a "haire couller water chamlett goune," and we read constantly of camlet cloaks till well into this century. I have found vast variety in the spelling of the word: chamelot, camblet, chamlett, camilet, as well as camlet.

CANTSLOPER. See SLOPS.

CAP. In Durfey's *Wit & Mirth*, or *Pills to Purge Melancholy*, there is a ballad on caps which proves that

> Any cap what e'er it be
> Is still the sign of some degree.

The author mentions

> The Monmouth cap, the saylors thrum
> And that wherein the tradesmen come ;
> The physicke, lawe, the cap divine.
> And that which crowns the Muses Nine.

Monmouth caps, worth two shillings each, were furnished to the Massachusetts colonists. These were much worn by seafaring men. We read, in *A Satyr on Sea Officers* "With Monmouth cap and cutlass at my side, striding at least a yard at every stride." Washington also ordered them as late as 1769. "Red mill'd capps," worth five pence apiece, were supplied to the Bay emigrants. The portraits of Endicott, Sewall, and many others, especially wig-haters, show black skull-caps. In the various Boston newspapers by the year 1740, we find advertised, "Strip'd and Scarlett Single & Double Worsted Caps, Round-puff't and Quilted Caps; Fine Imbroidered Velvett Caps, Kilmarnock Mill'd Caps, Thrumb'd Caps."

Women's caps were of equal variety by the middle of the century. We read of "Fly caps with Egrets, Drest Gauze Caps," round ear'd caps (which had no strings), strap caps (which had a strap under the chin). Bugle fly caps were worn in Pennsylvania about 1760. Mob caps were described as a caul with two lappets, and were much worn. They were slouchy, baggy caps, with floppy frills or ruffles — not elegant for full dress. Mr. Felt quotes a letter written from Cape Cod in 1720:

> Mobs are now worn but not so long by a quarter of a yard as mine. I was forced to cut mine half a quarter from each end to make them short enough for the fashion.

These mobs must have been the streamers upon the mob-caps. Ranelagh mobs were made of gauze or net, puffed about the head, with two ends crossed under the chin and then tied at the back, and left hanging in floating ends. The Queen's night-cap, though similar in shape, was made of richer gauze and was more trim and compact. It is familiar to us through having been worn by Martha Washington and shown in her portraits. It remained in fashion for nearly half a century.

See Biggin, Curch, Coif, Mercury.

Capuchin. A hooded cloak, so called from its resemblance to the hooded garment worn by the Capuchin monks. Fairholt,

Planché, and other English writers say capuchins were introduced into England in 1752, but this date is incorrect; the name appears in English publications as early as 1709. Fielding used it in "Tom Jones" in 1749, and the *Covent Garden Journal* of May 1, 1752, says:

> Within my memory the ladies covered their lovely necks with a Cloak, this was exchanged for the manteel, this again was succeeded by the pelorine, the pelorine by the neckatee, the neckatee by the capuchin which hath now stood its ground for a long time.

Even in America, in 1749, the *Boston Gazette* advertised "Cappechines." In June, 1753, Harriet Paine, the Boston shopkeeper, had "Flowered and Spotted Velvet for Capuchin Cloaks." Pink and figured mode capuchines, and colored and black silk, and black flowered mode for these cloaks came next, and were advertised in South Carolina newspapers. Fringe also appeared, and in 1767 crimson capuchin silk was worth four shillings and sixpence a yard. In order to show how rich a cloak and how richly trimmed these capuchins were, let me quote this notice from the *Boston Evening Post* of January 13, 1772:

> Taken from Concert Hall on Thursday Evening a handsom Crimson Satin Capuchin trimmed with a rich white Blond Lace with a narrow Blond Lace on the upper edge Lined with White Sarsnet.

Twelve dollars reward was offered for its return. They were for many years much worn by women of fashion, and were used as a riding-hood.

CARDINAL. A hooded cloak greatly worn during the first half of the eighteenth century. The name continued in use till this century. It was originally of scarlet cloth, like the mozetta of a cardinal; hence its name. Cardinals appear in Hogarth's prints, and are advertised in many New England papers for many years and in the *Maryland Gazette* in 1769.

CARSEY. See KERSEY.

CASSOCK. Steevens says a cassock "signifies a horseman's loose coat, and is used in that sense by the writers of the age of Shakespeare." It was apparently a garment much like a coat or jerkin, and the names were used interchangeably. It finally became applied only to the coat or gown of the clergy. In the "enuentory" of the goods supplied to the Piscataquay Plantations in 1635 are these items:

50	Cloth	Cassocks	&	breeches
153	Canvass	"	"	"
40	Shot	"	"	"

In the will of Robert Saltonstall, made in 1650, he names a "Plush Cassock," but cloth cassocks were the commonest wear. In the sixteenth century cassocks were worn by Englishwomen, but I have found no reference to their being worn by women in our colonies.

Castor. See Hat.

Catgut. A cloth woven in cords and used for lining and stiffening garments; and also I judge, from Mrs. Delany's reference to it, as a canvas for embroidery purposes.

John Adams, in his diary, under date 1766, tells of sitting to "hear the ladies talk of catgut, Paris net and riding-hoods." It was advertised in the newspapers until this century.

Caul. A caul was a net to confine the hair, or a flat-netted head-dress. The word is said to have been thus used from the Middle Ages to the seventeenth century. I find it thus employed in Virginia in 1642, in the inventory of one Richard Lusthead. As indicating the hinder portions of a woman's cap, the word was used till this century. It was also applied to one part of a wig.

Cherridary. This was an Indian cotton stuff much like a gingham. It was advertised for sale by the names cheridery, cherriderrey, charidery, from 1712 until Revolutionary times, and may have been cheap, as it often appears as the material of various articles of apparel of runaways; "cheridary wascotes," a "cherrederry gown," a "cherredary apron," &c. It is most frequently specified as being "narrow stript."

CIFFER.—See COIF.

CLOAK. This garment has been worn by both sexes from the time of the landing of the Cavaliers and Pilgrims. Ellinor Trasler had a sad-colored cloak in 1654. Another colonist had a "white Hair camblet Cloke lyned with blue." "Silk short Cloaks" were the wear in 1737, and in 1742 there were advertised in the *News Letter*: "Womens Cloaks of most Colours; viz: Scarlet, Crimson, Cloth Colour, made after the newest Fashion." Robert Saltonstall had a "gray cloke and a Sadd collered Cloke," and Major Pyncheon's "moehaire cloke" was worth one pound in 1703.

CLOGS. Clogs appear in newspaper advertisements from 1737 throughout the eighteenth century. In England the name was used as early as 1416. These overshoes were made of various materials. I find named for sale brocaded, leather-eared, leather-toed, silk, velvet-banded, worsted, black velvet, white damask, flowered silk and prunella clogs. The stilted soles were of wood or thick leather, and the upper bands were frequently made to match the shoes or slippers with which the clogs were intended to be worn. White damask clogs were certainly worthy the wear of a bride. Common clogs were worth in 1717 fifteen pence a pair, and in 1764 one shilling six pence a pair. Old clogs can be seen at the Deerfield Memorial Hall.

CLOUT. We read in *Hamlet:*

> a clout upon that head
> Where late the diadem stood;

and in *The Debate between Pride and Lowliness*,

> With homely clouts i-knitt upon their head
> Simple yet white as thing so coarse might be.

A clout was a coarse kerchief or covering for the head. I find the word in Maryland inventories.

COATS. I do not find coats named in the inventories of the goods and clothing furnished to the planters at Plymouth and at Massachusetts Bay; but the emigrants to the Piscataquay Plantations had "27 Lined Coats, 16 Moose Coats, and 15 Papous Coats," which latter garment, after frequent encounter in similar inventories and "painful" investigation and consideration, I have found to be pappoose coats. These would appear to be children's coats, but in a contemporary record I also find that "three papoose skins were equal in value to one beaver skin," so I wish to believe that the word papoose meant something other than an Indian baby. Josselyn said that moose-skin made "excellent coats for martial men," so doubtless the Piscataquay warriors wore the moose coats. The name and garment quickly came into vogue in Boston. Raccoon-skin coats were worn: one owned by Thomas Fenner of Windsor, Conn., was worth ten shillings. Until our own day huntsmen and frontiersmen wore deerskin coats or jackets, picturesque and appropriate garments. The Apostle Eliot received by the will of Joseph Weld in 1646 the gift of "a tawny cloth coat," and in the same year a neighbor, John Pope of Dorchester, bequeathed "two Vper Coates," which were overcoats

I fancy. In 1640 Robert Keayne of Boston paid "£2 10*s*. for a silver lac'd coat and a gold lac'd hat," while in the same year three plainer coats were worth the same amount.

Scarlet coats were plentiful in New England at that time, and Winthrop ordered in 1636 a coat of "sad foulding-colour without lace."

John Wynter, in 1636, had coats for the Indians that were worth "2 lb. Beaver" apiece. He writes to the consigner, "The coates are good, but somewhat of the shortest. The Indyans make choyse of the longest. They pass best."

The coat, as worn by men, is said by Fairholt to have originated from the long waistcoat, or vest as Pepys called it, worn in the reign of Charles II., and for many years it was straight and full-skirted. It was not sloped away at the sides till the time of George III.—until macaroni time. All drawings or descriptions of men's costumes assigned to earlier days should have square-skirted coats, save in the case of a soldier's uniform, which ere that date had been turned back in lapels or revers for convenience's sake, and held back by buttons. The memorandum of George Washington, given on page 40, shows the shape of coat which was fashionable in the middle of the century in America.

Horsemen's coats are frequently mentioned in early days; for instance, in the will of one Metcalfe, in 1664—"My largest gray Horseman's Coat." Gabriel Harris, of New London, had in 1684 a "Broadcloth Coat with Red lining & a white Serge coat," quite showy articles of attire. From advertisements of runaways we learn of the various names applied to various styles of coats. A deserter wore, in 1704, a "white cape cloth watchcoat;" a negro wore off in the same year "a Sad colour'd old Coat or new light Drugget coat with Buttons, Holes, and Linings of black;" another runaway had on a "Grego Watch Coat." Peter Faneuil bought in 1738 "2 Large Fine Well painted Beaver Coats," for sleighing. We read, under the date 1736, of the loss of a "Great Coat of Red Whitney with red velvet Cape. The Coat a little fully'd at the Back."

Perhaps the most curious name given to a

coat was one in the *Virginia Gazette* of May 2, 1757—"A Thunder and Lightning Coat; otherwise German Sarge."

Children wore coats. Judge Sewall appropriately gave one of "blew, faced with red," to a little Puritan Aaron. John Corwin paid, in 1679, six shillings for having a coat made for one of his children. Women wore coats also. The word was applied to their upper garments, and also to the petticoats, and it is often difficult to decide to which it refers. Sometimes it is thus used: "Petty Coats, Peti-cotes," or, as Sewall wrote it, "Petit-coats." The "turkey mohere coate" of Martha Emmons in 1666, the "blew shorte Coate, Green Vnder Coate, and Kersey Coate" of Jane Humphreys in 1668, were apparently outer garments. The "Silk Crape Quilted Coat" that runaway Keziah Wampum eloped with in 1740 seems somewhat difficult to place. See PETTICOAT.

COCKADE. The first naming of this word or article was in Rabelais, where it was written coquaide. In 1660 we read of cockarded hats. Steele and Pope wrote of cockards. Ribbon cockades were worn by women on hats and in the hair, as well as by men on cocked hats. In 1755 Horeshair "cocades" were advertised in the *Boston Evening Post;* then, gold, silver, lace, and wire cockades. Federalist cockades were roses of white and black ribbon.

Cockers. Also spelled cocurs, cocrez, and cokers. Laced high shoes or half-boots; also thick stocking legs without feet. The name is still used in England, as it was in Piers Ploughman's time, but is obsolete in New England.

Coif. I find the words coif, quoife, quoyf, quoiff, ciffer, coifer, quiffer, and quiff, all used in New England to refer to a close head-dress or cap. The words had applied originally to a hood or cap, equally for men's and women's wear, but appear in this country to have been used only for women's headgear. In a letter to Winthrop, dated 1636, we read of "cutt-worke coifes." And the Indian braves called English women

"Lazie Squaes" because they sat at home "embroidering coifs" instead of digging in the fields for their lords. Mary Haines's inventory in New London, in 1655, contained both the word ciffer and quoyf. Jane Humphrey left behind her in 1668 "a plain black Quoife without any lace, and my best quoife with a lace." John Pyncheon, of Springfield, sold in 1653 "blew coifers" to Henry Burt that were worth five shillings apiece." In Virginia the word was usually spelled quoiff.

Colchester Cloth. See Baize.

Colverteen. See Lace.

Comb. In the list of orders which John Eliot sent to England in 1651 he specified "4 Boxes of Combes" for the Indians, thus proving that he deemed cleanliness next to godliness. In 1737 Sir William Pepperell, ordering also for trade with the Indians, wished "I Grose Horn Combes, I Grose Ivory small teeth Combes." In 1763 in the *Boston Evening Post*, were advertised

"Fine Dander Combs, Horn & Buckling Combs, Touper Combs with & without Cases," and again, "Fine Dandriff Combs, and Tupee Cramber Combs." Ten years later came "Tortoise Shell Poll Combs, Ivory Tupee & Tail Combs," and then "Bent combs;" proving that they had—as I saw advertised in the *Connecticut Courant*—"combs of every denomination." I have seen an old case of tortoise-shell dressing combs about one hundred years old. The teeth were heavier and coarser than in our modern combs; hence perhaps their safe preservation to the present day.

The great "poll combs" of shell, horn or silver, for ornamenting the head are familiar to us all, and have been worn almost to the present day.

CORNET. Cotgrave said a cornet was "a fashion of Shadow or Boone grace vsed in old time and to this day by some old women," and Evelyn speaks of "the upper pinner of a cornet dangling about her cheeks like hounds ears." The head-covering of the Sisters of St. Vincent de Paul is called a cornet. Cornets and cornuted caps appear in early New York inventories, and were apparently a Dutch fashion.

COPPER-CLOUTS. See SPATTERDASHES.

CORSETS. See STAYS.

COURCHEF. Same meaning as curch, *q. v.*

CRAVAT. Blount in 1656 called a cravat "a new fashioned Gorget which women wear." Lawn cravats were advertised in the *Boston Evening Post* as early as 1753. The Governor of Acadia had lace cravats in 1690. Governor Berkeley, of Virginia, ordered in 1660 a cravat which was to cost five pounds. Such rich neck wear as that could not have been found in New England at that date. In the middle of the eighteenth century we often read of "black mill'd cravats."

CREWELL. Fine worsted used originally for fringe and garters, then for embroidery purposes.

CROCUS. There is no clew whatever to the

quality of this stuff, though the word was for a century in common use. Nor does the definition of the word in this sense appear in any English or American dictionary. A runaway slave was advertised in the *Boston News Letter* of October, 1704, as wearing a "Crocus Apron;" others in the *Virginia Gazette* of 1757 with "Crocus Trowzers." In a crazily wild letter written from the Barbadoes by Richard Hall to Benning Wentworth in 1719, he says of smuggling, "This is indeed to squint over the Left Shoulder, to run Crocus under a wrapper of Ozenbrigs," which would seem to imply that crocus was a fine and costly fabric. Still, "trowzers" at that date were made wholly of coarse linen and tow stuffs, not of rich or heavy materials. Miss Caroline Hazard in her interesting account of Narragansett colonial days—*College Tom*—gives many valuable household inventories. From them we learn that in 1760 the cost of weaving crocus was but half that of weaving flannel; which would also imply that crocus was a cheap coarse stuff. Its general wear by slaves and servants would point to the same conclusion.

CROSSCLOTH. A crosscloth was a portion of a woman's head-dress worn with a coif in the seventeenth century, and was apparently the same as a forehead cloth. I find "crossecloths" enumerated with quoifes in the possessions of Richard Lusthead in Maryland in 1642. A Puritan of Wenham, Mass., and another of Dorchester had them in 1647. Hence, they were worn by both Puritan and Cavalier dames.

CURCH. This word, as used in New England and in Pennsylvania, designated an inner cap for the head, worn by women, and usually of plain linen. It is doubtless an abbreviation of kerchief, and is of Scotch origin. It is frequently used by Scott in his novels, and a note in *The Lady of the Lake* says, "The snood was exchanged for the curch, toy, or coif, when a Scottish lass passed by marriage into the matron state."

CUSTALL. See STAYS.

CUTWORK.

> "Cut werke was greate both in court and tounes,
> Both in menes hoddis and also in their gounes."

A portrait of Louis of Anjou shows him

dressed in a hood, surtout, and a long shoulder sash all edged with cutwork—a graceful openwork embroidery in the shape of leaves. The excessive use of cutwork embroidery was forbidden to the Puritans, yet cutwork coifs were worn in the new land. Christopher Youngs, of Wenham, Mass., owned them in 1647; and one writer complained of the vanity of the Pilgrims in sending to England for cutwork. The Massachusetts Indians noted, as did Burton in his *Anatomy of Melancholy*, that English women loved to occupy their time with embroidering cutwork. In several of the century-darkened portraits of our ancestors that have descended to us, especially of the Virginian settlers, the broad collars appear to have cutwork borders.

Cypress. Also cyprus, cipre, sipers, sypress, syphus. Originally a rich stuff, cloth of gold and silk, the name came to be applied only to a thin mourning silk which was used like crape, and was in substance much like crape. Phillips in 1678 said cypress was "a fine curled stuff part Silk part Hair, of a Cobweb thinness, of which hoods for Women are made." It was named in a New England will as early as 1695—"half a piece of sipers." It was always black. Autolycus in *The Winter's Tale* says,

> Lawne as white as driven snow,
> Cyprus black as ere was crow.

"Silk Crape, Widow's Crape, Cyprus and Hat Crape" were advertised in the *Boston Evening Post* of 1755, and until Federal days.

DAMASK. A rich fabric woven in elaborate patterns in silk, silk and wool, or linen; and when in silk, frequently of various colors. In 1698 a piece of damask was said to be worth £2 10*s*. This may have been a fabric of linen or of silk. We read of "India Flower'd Damask and Venetian Flower'd Damask," which were surely silk. Negro women ran off in green flowered damask gowns and red damask petticoats, which were probably woollen damask. By Revolutionary times, in the *Connecticut Courant* we read of "silk and cotton Damascusses" which were evidently also damask, and of "Damascuss for Waistcoats." Many of the rich garments of the times were of damask, and the materials of our own day are not superior either in design or color to these colonial fabrics. The gorgeous gowns of Peter Faneuil's sister, which are preserved in cases and exhibited at the Boston Art Museum, are good examples.

Dauphiness. This was the name of a certain style of mantle. Harriott Paine had "Dauphiness Mantles" for sale in Boston in 1755.

Demicastor. See Hat.

Desoy. The full name of this material was sergedesoy, or sergedusoy,—a coarse silken stuff, as the name plainly indicates. It was in frequent use in the eighteenth century, especially for men's coats and waistcoats.

Dimity. This ribbed cotton stuff is said to have been made first at Damietta. It was mentioned by the Apostle John Eliot as early as 1651, on the list of goods ordered from England. "White Dimity," "Corded Dimothy," "Flowered dymmitty," appear at later dates in colonial papers. In fact, the material has been used until the present day.

DORNEX. A heavy, coarse linen, much like canvas, originally made at Dorneck or Tournay. It appears on lists under various spellings: dornix, tornix, darnex, darnick, dorneck, dornickes. In 1658 Simon Eire, of Boston, had a bed with "curtaince and valence of Dornix." In 1652 Thomas Olliver had a "dornix carpitt." It was too coarse and stiff for wear for gentlefolk, but servants had garments made of it. I read of "darnex petticoats," "dornix breeches," and frequently of "dornex jackets," on negro house-servants.

DOUBLET. A name apparently given because the garment was at first of double material, wadded between. It was frequently belted and made without sleeves, and was originally used as an outer garment worn over a waistcoat, and worn with long hose. In the "apparell for one hundred men" furnished in 1628 by the Massachusetts Bay Company, were "200 sutes of Norden dussens or hampsheere kersies lyned the hose with skins, the dublet with lynen of gilford or gedlyman kerseys 2*s.* 10*d.* to 3*s.* a yard, 4½ yards to a sute." Hence it is evident that doublet and hose formed a suit. Richard Sawyer, of Hartford had, in 1648, "bucks-leather, calfs-leather and liver-colour'd and musck-coulour'd cloth doublitts." Zerubbabel Endicott, of Salem, left by will in 1683 a "black coat with Doublet and Hose." In the Southern colonies doublets were much more the mode than in New England, and of richer material—"satten doubletts with silver buttons" and velvet doublets.

Doublets were also worn by women. Stubbs says, "Though this be a kind of attire proper only to a man, yet they blush not to wear it." Pepys, in 1666, sharply criticises English women for wearing doublets. Witch Anne Hibbins, of Boston, had a black satin one worth ten shillings. I do not find doublets named in inventories of the eighteenth century, except in one or two cases. Major John Pyncheon, an old Springfield gentleman who died in 1703, left behind him "a Light coulour'd Dublet with gold twist, and sad coulour'd Britches."

Dowlas. A heavy linen largely imported from earliest times — the "dowlas, filthy dowlas" of Falstaff's day. It was made in Brittany. Governor Barefoot, of New Hampshire, sent in 1688 for "as many yards of Doulas as will make a dozen shirts." John Wynter imported in 1638 "6 Doz Dowlys Shurtes at 4*s.* 4*d.* one with the other." The name appears in occasional use until this century, usually applied to the material of shirts or summer breeches.

Drawboys. In the *Boston Gazette* of May, 1750, we read of "Fine Figured Drawboys for Womens Coats with Fringe."

Drawers. Cotgrave says that coarse stockings made to draw on over other hose were called drawers. Leathern drawers were supplied to each Boston emigrant, and were, I think, draw-strings for the knee-bands of breeches. I find the word seldom used in New England in its present signification in the seventeenth century. In New York, gentlemen had silk and calico drawers, which were probably summer breeches.

DRUGGET. A fabric of wool worth twelve shillings a yard in 1713, and much used for heavy petticoats and coats.

DUCAPE. This was a heavy silk of plain color corded somewhat like our modern Ottoman silk. As early as 1675 Hull ordered to be brought on the Seaflower "Black Ducape & Lustrings." It was advertised by milliners and merchants for many years, frequently under the name Duc Cape. To show its wearing powers (or the painstaking care of our grandmothers), let me give the experience of Elizabeth Porter, whose wedding gown in 1770 was brown ducape. Eighteen years later this ducape gown was made over, and forty years from the wedding-day it was still in existence and sound enough to be again refashioned.

DUFFELS. "Duffle" was woollen stuff originally made in Duffel, a town in Flanders. It was excluded from England for a time, to favor home manufactures. It had a thick tufted or knotted nap. De Foe said this stuff was made at Whitney, England, purposely for winter wear in America. Certainly "coats of duffels" are constantly mentioned. The match-coats sold to the Indians were made of it, and it supplanted fur garments and in time affected the fur trade. In the *Colonial Documents of New York* I read, "Duffel cannot be called cloth, it is worse than a sorte called wadmoll, and not ever worne by any Christians, only by the Indians."

We find Hull ordering "Dutch Duffals white, blue and striped" in 1672, and Sewall "good steel blew duffal" a few years later. Wait Winthrop writes to his brother in 1675, "The Duffels is none of the best but tis cheape at 4 shilling a yard; the best is 5*s.* 6*d.* or six shilling." William Byrd, of Virginia, writing in 1683 said, "The Duffields is the worst I ever saw . . . Coler too light, a Darker blue pleases better." Duffels formed so large a part of a trader's stock that the name finally became a general term applied to the entire outfit of a sportsman or camper.

DURANT. A close-grained woollen stuff, so named from its strength and wearing qualities. Among many advertisements of it I will note but one—in the *Connecticut Courant* of April 22, 1776.

DUSSENS. Sometimes spelled dozens. The Bay planters were furnished "100 sutes of Norden dussens or Hampshire kersies." Dussens was a kersey, *q. v.*

EAR-RINGS. The earliest portraits of colonial women display no ear-rings. The widow of Colonel Livingstone of New London had a "pair of stoned ear-rings" in 1735. In the *Boston Evening Post* of June 1755 we read of "Undressed Ear-rings, Stone, French-Pearl & Crincled Ear-rings, French Rose Ear-rings and Cristiall Ear-rings"—so they evidently had become at that date wholly the mode. In 1771 J.

Coolidge, Jr., had still further styles—"Paste, enamelled, pearl, garnet, mock garnet and black ear-rings." In the *Connecticut Courant* of May, 1775, we read this notice: "For the Ladies: Pierc'd & Plain stone ear-rings set in gold & silver; jointed gold wires for the ears." Bernard Gratz had for sale in Philadelphia in 1760: "Fancy cluster ear-rings; French pearl, circled and points; plain open ear-rings; Garnet night ear-rings."

EGRET. Sometimes spelt aigret. A tuft of feathers worn by women for a head ornament. We read of bugle, silk, and silver egrets, and fly caps with egrets, in the *Boston Evening Post* of November, 1755, and for thirty years later, as long as military fashions prevailed.

ELAMOD. See ALAMODE.

ELLAPINE. See ALLAPINE.

EQUIPAGE. An ornamental case for women's wear to hold scissors, knife, thimble, pencil, tooth-pick case, tweezers, "ear-pick," bodkin, nail-cleaner, etc. In the time of George I. an equipage was worn hooked to the left side. At a later date it was hung by a stay hook on the upper edge of the bodice. I find "Silver Equipages" advertised in the *Boston News Letter* of April 28, 1768, and steel equipages also. See Etui.

Erminetta. A thin stuff for summer wear. In the *Boston Evening Post* of 1751 we read, "Genteel Linen and Cotton Erminettas." Runaway negresses were advertised as wearing off erminetta gowns.

Ermozen. See Armozine.

Estamine. See Taminy.

Etui. This was a name synonymous with equipage. In the *Salem Gazette*, in 1784, were named, "Ladies Neat House wifs and Etwees." Isaiah Thomas, in his Book Catalogue of about the same date advertised "Ladies Elegant Red Morocco Huswives and Etwees with Silver Locks and Some Silver mounted. Red Morocco Pocket books with Etwees." I have never found it spelled etui until modern times, but frequently estuy, ettwee, etuy, etc. See EQUIPAGE.

FALLING BAND.

> The eighth Henry (as I understand)
> Was the first king that ever wore a Band
> And but a Falling-Band, plaine with a hem
> All other people knew no use of them.

Thus wrote old John Taylor in his *Praise of Clean Linnen.*

The broad, plain linen collar, turned down over the neck of the doublet or jerkin, was the common form of the falling-band. It is familiar to us through early portraits. It sometimes consisted of several pieces, or collars, one falling over the other. It was frequently called simply a fall. Both names appear in a majority of the early colonial inventories. The "three Yards ffine Lace for ffrills and ffals" which Governor Berkeley, of Virginia, ordered in 1660, and which were worth £2 8*s.*, may have been intended for falls, or for fallals, which latter were ornamental knots of lace and ribbon worn in England that I have never seen specially named elsewhere in American inventories or lists. See Band.

Fan. The first newspaper advertisement in New England relating to fans was in the *Boston News Letter* of April, 1714. On July 18th, 1728, this notice appeared:

George Harding lately from London, now at Mr. John Potters, Confectioners, Mounteth all sorts of Fans as well as any Done in old England. He likewise hath a large Sortment of Curious Mounts which he will dispose of very Reasonably, not purposing to stay long in These Parts.

By 1732 other fan mounters had come to town, and set up business on Beacon street, near the Common.

The Person that mounts Fans having a Parcel Just arriv'd. All Gentlewomen that Desire to be Supply'd may have them. She intending to Mount no more desires they would be speedy in Coming.

Perhaps a few wealthy Boston dames may have owned fans from earliest Colonial days. Abigail Kellond paid £5 for one in Boston, in 1686; but certainly fans were not commonly used until toward the middle of the eighteenth century. Feather fans with gold handles had been too purely court luxuries to be plentiful in the new land, though the "2 Feather Skreens" in Madam Usher's wardrobe in 1725 were doubtless hand screens or fans. In 1736 "Women's & Children's Ivory, Cocoa & Bone Stick't Fans" were advertised, and "Fine Paper Fans," and "Rich Fans of Leather & Paper Mounts."

The *London Magazine* of 1744 speaks of fans at that date as wonderfully increased in size, "from three quarters of a foot to a foot and three quarters or two feet;" and I presume the fashion spread to America. In 1750 women's and children's mourning and half mourning and church fans were offered for sale, thus showing a fine and discriminating regard for fashion. "Paddlestick cut silver mount fans" appeared in 1764, and "Marlborough & other fashionable fans." Occasionally a portrait of this date is shown of a fan-bearing dame, and a few of such fans have been preserved to us, looking more of the French taste than of the English.

FARRANDINE. See FERRANDINE.

FEARNAUGHT. A thick cloth with a long pile, also called dreadnaught and fear-nothing. In the *Virginia Gazette* in 1752 and 1753 we frequently read of runaway slaves wearing fearnothing jackets.

FERRANDINE. Also farrandine and farendon. A cloth partly of silk, partly of wool or hair, much like what we now call poplin. It was frequently named by Pepys and was much worn at that time, and was used specially for waistcoats. The name appears in New York and New England lists of clothing.

FERRET. Originally a narrow worsted ribbon or tape used for bindings. The word ferret or ferriting was at a later date applied to any narrow tape, such as shoe lacing. In the *Boston News Letter* of 1762 "Cotton and Silk Ferrit Laces, also Black and Colour'd Silk Ferrits" were advertised. The word will occasionally be seen on tape-boxes in old shops nowadays.

FILEMOT. A corruption of feuille-morte —of the color of a dead leaf.

FOOT-MANTLE. See SAFEGUARD.

FRIEZE. A coarse woollen stuff worn by poor folk, and used since the fourteenth century. I have seen the word but rarely in colonial inventories. The New Hampshire settlers had "ffrise" garments.

FROG. An ornamental cloak, coat, or hat button. Frogs are seen on few of the early portraits. Governor Belcher wears a coat trimmed with them in his portrait. Major John Pyncheon had, in 1703, a "light coulour'd cape-coat with Frogs on it." In the *New England Weekly Journal* of 1736 "New Fashion'd Frogs" are named; and later, "Spangled Scalloped & Brocaded Frogs." Frogs also appeared on the list of hat trimmings.

FROSTS. Judge Sewall wrote on Jan. 19, 1717: "Great Rain and very Slippery; was fain to wear Frosts." These frosts were perhaps what have been called on horses "frost nails," or calks, and at a later date, for men's wear, calks. They were simply spiked soles to help the wearer to walk on ice. A pair may be seen at the Deerfield Memorial Hall.

FURBELOWS. In the *Pleasant Art of Money-Catching* (1730) a furbelowed scarf is said "not to be purchased under as much money as heretofore would have bought a good citizen's wife a new gown and petticoat. But these furbelows are not confin'd to scarfs, but they must have furbelow'd gowns and furbelow'd petticoats, and, as I have heard, furbelow'd smocks too."

Furbelows were invented by a Frenchman named Langlée, the son of a waiting-maid of Madame de Maintenon, and were simply rows of quilled flounces, and subsequently gathered flounces looped in clusters of plaits. They were called in France falbalas. Furbelowed gowns and petticoats and scarfs our foremothers had in America, and perhaps the other garment also. Furbelowed collars we read of. The "Furbelow'd Gold Gauze

Scarf" of Richard Hall's wife (that he sold in Boston after her death at the Barbadoes) must have been beautiful, indeed. I have seen no notice of the English "rump furbelows," nor of the brooches placed in these furbelows and called "rump jewels" or rumphlets; but I doubt not that wealthy New England dames were thus bedizened.

FUSTIAN. A stout twilled cotton stuff worth, in 1640, a shilling a yard, and much used for jackets and petticoats.

GARTERS. To the planters of the Massachusetts Bay Colony were furnished "10 dussen peare of Norwich garters, about 5*s*. a dussen pr." At an early date in the affairs of the colony, silk garters were prohibited as an extravagant vanity. Susannah Oxenbridge, the widow of the rich Boston minister, specified and bequeathed in her will in 1695, "My best Silke Stockins & Garters." In the *Boston Independent Advertiser* of 1748 "Gartrings" appear, and in 1769, in the *Boston Evening Post*, were named "Cord Chain Thread & Knee Garters," and also

"London Turkey & Scotch Gartrings," and "Lettered Garters." So it is evident that garters were quite an important addition to dress, and possibly an expensive one too. In the list of household goods and clothing which the Governor of Arcadia asserted that "Mr. Phips," the Governor of Massachusetts, had stolen from him, or deprived him of, were four pair of silken garters; with which borrowed finery possibly Governor Phips cut a fine figure. Judge Sewall had a rare pair of garters given to him in 1688—"a pair of Jerusalem Garters which cost above 2 pieces 8 (Spanish dollars) in Algeria." Snakeskin garters were worn to ward off cramp in the leg.

GINGERLINE. Among the stuffs supplied to the Indians we find gingerline. The traders paid one yard and a half of gingerline for a bearskin, so doubtless many a brave wore gay gingerline breeches, and many a squaw a gingerline jacket. In the Duke of Newcastle's comedy, *The Triumphant Widow*, 1677, one character wears a "gingerline cloth cloke with olive plush cape."

The word occurs in the Massachusetts Archives as late as 1703.

GIRDLE. Gold and silver girdles were among the articles of dress forbidden by the Massachusetts General Court in 1634. In 1628 "lether girdles" were assigned to each male emigrant. In later days they appear frequently in inventories, usually of buff leather. Susannah Oxenbridge had a "large Silke Girdle" in 1695. It was not till 1755 that silver girdles and girdle buckles were advertised for sale. The *Weekly Rehearsal*, of Jan. 10, 1732, says, "in the Present Custom no Girdle terminates the Wast," and seems to regard the absence of that confining adornment as very indiscreet and almost immoral. In New York the girdle was universally worn by women of Dutch descent or birth. It was usually a rich ornament, being made of silver—sometimes of gold—and to it were hung the housewife's bunch of keys, her silver-clasped Bible, and frequently an "equipage."

GLOVES. Nearly all the portraits of the settlers,—Puritans, Cavaliers, and Quakers—

display gloves. Governors Endicott and Rawson wear rich gloves with deep embroidered cuffs or gauntlets. Zerubbabel Endicott left fringed gloves by will in 1683. They were imported in large numbers even in early days, and were of various materials; "cordevant, buckskin, shammy, sattin, Irish lamb and glazed lambs-wool." Silver and gold fringed gloves also were worn, and "Pompedore" gloves. In 1628 gloves were furnished to the planters. One hundred men had "16 dussen of gloves of which 12 dussen of calfs leather, 2 dussen of sheeps leather, 2 dussen Kyd." Gloves for women and children appear in all lists of wares in the newspapers. One great expense of a funeral was the gloves. In some communities these were sent as an approved and elegant form of invitation to relatives and friends and dignitaries, whose presence was desired. In the case of a funeral of any person prominent in state, church, or society, vast numbers of gloves were disbursed; "none of 'em of any figure but what had gloves sent to 'em." At the funeral of the wife of Governor Belcher, in 1736, over one thousand pairs of gloves were given away; at the funeral of Andrew Faneuil three thousand pairs; the number frequently ran up to several hundred, as at the funerals of some of the New York patroons. Different qualities of gloves were presented at the same funeral to persons of different social circles, or of varied degrees of consanguinity or acquaintance. Frequently the orders for these *vales* were given in wills. As early as 1633 Samuel Fuller, of Plymouth, directed in his will that his sister was to have gloves worth twelve shillings; Governor Winthrop and his children each "a paire of gloves of five shillings;" while plebeian Rebecca Prime had to be contented with a cheap pair worth two shillings sixpence.

The under-bearers who carried the coffin were usually given different and cheaper gloves than were the pall-bearers. We find seven pairs of gloves given at a pauper's funeral. Of course the minister, clergyman, or dominie always was given gloves; they were showered on him at weddings, christenings, funerals.

Various kinds of gloves are specified as

suitable for mourning; for instance, in the *Boston Independent Advertiser* in 1749, and in New York newspapers of the same date, "Black Shammy Gloves and White Glazed Lambs Wool Gloves suitable for Funerals." White gloves were as often given as black, and purple gloves also. Good specimens of old mourning gloves have been preserved in the cabinets of the Worcester Society of Antiquity.

By Liberty Days, in 1769, even mourning gloves showed the influences of the times, and were made in America of American materials, and it was proposed that they be stamped with a suggestive design such as the Liberty Tree.

GLOVE TIGHTENS. The long gloves worn by women were held up at the elbows by various devices. Glove-tightens made of plaited horse-hair were a favorite method. Glove strings were of enough importance and value for the sister of wealthy Peter Faneuil to send her discarded ones to London to be sold. Roses and ties of narrow ribbon were also worn at glove-tops. "Elastick glove-tops" were advertised in the *Salem Gazette* of July 29, 1789. These glove fasteners were also called glove-bands, and in the *Charleston Gazette* (S. C.) of July 9, 1760, we read of hair glove-tops, probably made of braided horse-hair.

GOLBERTAINE. See LACE.

GOLOSH. A "galage" was a shoe "which has nothing on the feet but a latchet." A golosh was a shoe with soles of wood or leather, with straps to keep it on the foot. It was worn over an ordinary shoe or slipper in bad weather. They were used at an early date, for in February, 1687, Judge Sewall notes: "Sent my mothers Shoes & Golowshoes to carry to her." In 1736 Peter Faneuil sent to England for "Galoushoes" for his sister. I find them advertised in the *New England Weekly Journal* in 1739, and from that date in varying intervals in various papers, till 1776. The popular spelling was "golo-shoe" pronounced as written, not in a single word, golosh. Occasionally it was written "golossians." See CLOGS and PATTENS.

GORGET. An ornamental neckband which was very full and broad in front. The word is found but seldom in colonial records, and only in Maryland and Virginia. In 1642, one wealthy Maryland planter left behind him at his death a large number of laced gorgets.

GRAIN. A color—scarlet. The word is so used by Shakespeare, Spenser, and Milton. It was derived from the grain-like insects of the cochineal. I read in New England inventories of waistcoats of grain.

GRAZZETS. A dress-stuff appearing in lists in the *News Letter* from 1712 to 1768, often specified as "changeable grazzets."

GRIDELIN. Also gresdelin, gredolin, grisetin. From the French *gris de lin*—flax-gray. A gray-violet color which was fashionable in the eighteenth century.

GROGRAM. Govenor Winthrop wrote thus: "I purpose to send by the bearer a piece of Turkey Grogram, about ten yards, to make you a suit." It was a stiffened stuff of silk and wool, much like heavy mohair, and had, it is said, a diagonal weave. Captain Clayborne of Palmer's Island, Maryland, had a "stitcht Grogram doublett" in 1638. We read until Revolutionary times of grogram waistcoats and cloaks, and sometimes of garments of silk grograham. We find Governor Belcher writing to his London tailor, in 1733, about a "yellow grogram suit work't strong as well as neat and curious."

HAIR-CLASPS. These ornaments for the hair—clasps to hold up the braided back hair—were advertised for sale in the New York newspapers and in the *Connecticut Courant* of January, 1791, and were worn until a simpler form of hair-dressing appeared about the year 1800. They were usually rather a cheap ornament, set with paste jewels, as was the fashion of the day, with marcasite, garnet, pearl and mocho stones; or made of silver-gilt. I have also seen them of cut-steel, now tarnished and rusty with years.

HAIR-LACE. A fillet or ribbon for tying up the hair. Universally worn by women of all ranks and stations in the eighteenth century.

Hair-Peg. See Bodkin.

Hair-pin. In November, 1755, I find the first notice of hair-pins for sale—at Harriot Paine's in Boston. She was a great importer of novelties to fair Bostonians. Previously to that time New England dames may have skewered the hair, for aught I know. Indeed, as she advertised "Double & Single Hairpins" in June, 1775, the single hair-pins may have been simply a long skewer of strong wire. Hairbins and hairbines and harepins and black hairpens appear later, sandwiched in among the names of woollen goods, so the articles—or possibly they may be stuffs—thus designated were doubtless plentiful enough. I do not find hair-pins on wigmakers' and barbers' lists, in any colonial newspapers; and I find some indications that hairbine was the name of a woollen material. See Bodkin.

Haling-Hands. These were heavy gloves or mittens of woolen stuff or felting (for we read complaints of their being moth-eaten), and were frequently sent to the colonists at Richmond Island, Maine, for use on the fishing vessels. The evident signification of the word points to their being used as hand coverings for sailors and workmen while hauling cables or doing other heavy work; and they are still sold and thus used. They were frequently lined in the palms with leather or heavy cloth. We read of a Maine workman, in 1639, buying "six paire haling-hands & 1 yard 3-4 Cape Cloth to lyne them & to make myttinges." Another fisherman bought "list to lyn halings." These haling-hands sold for about sixpence a pair.

HANDKERCHIEF. In the inventory of the goods supplied to the one hundred planters of Massachusetts Bay, in 1628, were items of "200 hankerchers" and "ells of sheer lynnen for hankerchers." At that time they were also called muckinders in England. In the early wills "handkerchiefes" were mentioned among articles of importance, and they were doubtless handsome and of rich materials, such as the handkerchief that

Richard Hull sent from Barbadoes to be sold in Boston, "one silke Handkerchief with Gold Edging." They were not all of silk or linen, the "handkerchiefs that India's shuttle boast" came quickly into the market with the increased Oriental trade. As early as 1737 good patriotic Peter Faneuil smuggled into port 62 dozen Romall handkerchiefs at £7 a dozen; and in 1755 "Lemone Handkerchiefs" were advertised in the *Boston Gazette*. These were of the India cotton material lemmanee. In the same paper at the same time were "Scotch and Paistwork Handkerchiefs." "Birdsey'd" and "Sarsnet" are the next names of the stuffs of which handkerchiefs were made, and November 18, 1767, one Boston shopkeeper had "linen check'd spotted flower'd stamp'd & border'd Cambrick; Barcelona, Pullicat, Lungee, Bandanoe, China, Culgee, Negligee, Rosett & Sattinet Handkerchiefs" which—with the Bandanoet and Bilboa handkerchiefs of Jolley Allen's shop form a list we could hardly equal in modern times. And these were not all; in the same year in the *Connecticut Courant* a lost box was advertised. It contained "One plain gauze handkerchief lac'd, spotted gauze handkerchief lac'd with a plain blond lace, two plain gauze handkerchiefs." These latter and the "black gauze yard wide Handkerchiefs" of the same date must, I fancy, have been used as neckkerchiefs. Abigail Adams, writing in 1785, to Mrs. Storer said: "Abby has made you a miniature handkerchief just to show you one mode; but caps hats and handkerchiefs are as various as ladies and milliners fancies can devise." These handkerchiefs were also ornamental neckerchiefs.

Rebecca Franks, writing from New York to Philadelphia in 1778, also sent a handkerchief to show the pattern.

HAT. Each emigrant was allowed by the Massachusetts Bay Company, in 1628, one "black hatt lyned at the brow with lether." This was apparently the best head-gear of the colonists, perhaps used only for Sunday and funeral wear. In 1634 a law was passed in Massachusetts against the wearing of beaver hats save by wealthy men. It apparently availed little, though men were prosecuted under it, for beaver hats were worn from that day as long as beaver hats were made — and nominally much longer. The colonists apparently believed, like the author of *Merry Drolleries* in 1661,

> Of all the felts that may be felt
> Give me the English beaver.

Doubtless the high price of such head coverings was the chief objection in the mind of the frugal magistrates. Beaver hats cost from four to six pounds apiece in England, as we learn from Pepys and other contemporary diarists. Hence it is no wonder that when owned at all in a frontier province, like New England or even Virginia, they were valuable enough to be left by bequest and given as tokens of friendship and respect. In 1694 black beaverettes were worth two pounds apiece in America, while castor hats cost but thirty-one shillings. A demi-castor was worth £1 6*s.* in Springfield in 1658. In Maryland and Virginia rich head-gear was worn; hats with gold hat-bands and feathers.

In 1650 Robert Saltonstall left a "black beavor hatt" by will; in 1633 Samuel Fuller left his "best Hatt" to his minister, Elder Brewster. Hats were also made of cloth. In the tailor's bill of work done for Jonathan Corwin, of Salem, in 1679, we read, "To making a Broadcloath Hatt 14*s*. To making 2 hatts & 2 jackets for your two sonnes 19*s*." In 1672 an association of Massachusetts hatters asked privileges and protection from the colonial government, to aid and encourage American manufacture, but they were refused until they made better hats. Shortly after, however, the exportation of raccoon fur to England was forbidden, or taxed, as it was found to be useful in the home manufacture of hats.

Castor hats were largely imported; Pepperell ordered six dozen from England in one invoice. They appear on the heads of runaways in many an advertisement. Cocked hats came in vogue in New England when they did in England, and varied widely in shape as they did in looping, sometimes being turned up only in front with a button, at other times having three laps. In 1670 hat brims were about six inches wide. Dr. Holyoke said that in 1732 his father wore one seven inches wide. In 1742 it became

> a fashionable whim
> To wear it with a narrow brim.

Cocked hats were richly trimmed with metal laces, cords, caddis, ferret, buttons, ribbons, cockades, rosettes, and were also painted. In 1738 in the *Boston News Letter* runaways were advertised, one wearing a "hat painted of several colours;" another a hat "painted red." The words colored and painted appear to have been used interchangeably in the eighteenth century; and "colour'd hats" are frequently named. Cocked hats were worn by civilians until this century, and by the army also. During the Revolutionary War the sentence of whipping with five lashes was imposed on any soldier whose hat was found carelessly unlooped—"uncockt"—as it "gave him a hang-dog look."

Puritan women also wore felt and beaver and castor hats, and bequeathed them by will, as did the men. A letter written in

Dorchester by a lover to his lass, in 1647, tells of "thinking upon you for a hat & chose out ye comelyest fashion hatt yt they could find avoiding fantastick fashions. Ye hatt was a demi-castor the priz was 24*s*."

Though Mary Harris, of New London, named a "straw hatt" in her will in 1655, such mention is unusual, and would have been in England at the same date. On June 18, 1727, the *New England Weekly Journal* advertised "Women's Hatts made of fine Bermuda Platt." An affectation of country innocence made straw hats fashionable at about this time in England, where they were called "Churchills." In 1732, a writer in the *Weekly Rehearsal*, speaks thus of "High-Croun'd Hats," "After being confin'd to Cots & Villages so long a time, they have become the Mode of Quality & the politest Distinction of a Fashionable Undress." In 1742, in April, in the *Boston Evening Post*, fine Leghorn straw hats for women were advertised at sixteen to fifty shillings apiece, and a "parcel of fine Ruff'd hats" for ladies. In 1737 Boston milliners had "New Fashion'd Nonpareil'd feather'd Hatts for ladies," which must have been mighty fine. In 1751 Harriot Paine had for sale "Saxon blue silk and Hair Hatts, black horsehair & Leghorn hatts," and in 1753 "Black & white & Black Horsehair Hatts emboss'd and stampt Sattin Hatts." "Fine beverett hats with tabby linings," "tissue sattin & chipt hatts," were also sold in South Carolina as well as the more northern States. We gain a little suggestion of contemporary historical events by the names, "Quebeck Hats and Garrick Hats." We know prices also: "Womens chipt Hats 60*s*. O.T. per doz." in 1764, and "4*s*. 6*d* apiece O.T." in 1767. In the latter year plain-trimmed and skeleton hats appear; on April 16, 1773, "Ladies Newest Fashion White Beaver Riding Hats." These riding hats had previously been denounced as an exceeding affectation in a "riding equipage."

The *Salem Gazette* advertised in July, 1784, "Air Balloon" and "Princess" hats. These were French fashions. A large brimmed hat was fashionable for some time at this date; it had a low soft silk or gauze crown and a broad ribbon bow with long ends at the back, and was trimmed with three ostrich feathers. Emily and Marlborough hats appeared in 1786. Another modish hat had a brim without a crown. In 1796 Sally McKean (afterward Marquise d'Yrigo) wrote thus, to the sister of Dolly Madison, of the fashions of her day :

> The hats are quite different shape from what they used to be ; they have no slope in the crown ; scarce any rim, and are turned up at each side and worn very much on the side of the head. Several of them are made of chipped woods commonly known as cane hats ; they are all lined. One that has come for Mrs. Bingham is lined with white and trimmed with broad purple ribbon put around in large puffs, with a bow on the left side.

Hive. In milliners' lists in Massachusetts and Pennsylvania the word is seen, and it was applied to a straw head-covering shaped like a bee-hive for women's wear. Shakespeare, in the *Lover's Complaint*, wrote ;

> Upon her head a platted hive of straw
> Which fortified her visage from the sun.

In Durfey's *Wit and Mirth, or Pills to purge Melancholy*, he speaks, in a ballad on caps, of a "satin and a velvet hive for men's wear." I have also read in American newspapers of the eighteenth century, in the tedious romances that occasionally may be found in their columns, of fine young country maids wearing hives on their heads.

Hood. Though English prints of the seventeenth century usually represent Puritan women in steeple-crowned, straight-brimmed, untrimmed woollen hats, as ugly and unbecoming as those of their sober spouses, I firmly believe that our Pilgrim mothers made their ocean journey and landed on Plymouth Rock in hoods; and hoods did their descendants constantly wear in spite of the meddlesome prohibition of silk and tiffany hoods by the early magistrates. Throughout the other colonies they were also worn by women of every station. Through the two centuries following came a brilliant inflorescence of hoods; though sometimes under other names. In 1666 Ann Clarke and Jane Humphrey, of Dorchester, left hoods by will. In 1695 Susannah Oxenbridge specified in her will her "Scarlett colour'd hoode & a black hoode." These hoods were not always of heavy materials. In New York, women had "love-hoods" of silk and gauze—a pretty name and I am sure a pretty covering. In 1712 Richard Hall sent, from Barbadoes to Boston, a trunk of his deceased wife's finery to be sold, among which was "one black Flowered Gauze Hoode," and he added rather spitefully that he "could send better but it would be too rich for Boston." Servants wore hoods also; many runaways were advertised as wearing that head-gear; on May 6, 1717, the *Boston News Letter* contained a description of a gayly attired Indian runaway, who wore off a "Camblet Ryding Hood fac'd with blue;" while another wore a dark brown riding-hood lined and faced with crimson. A riding-hood had apparently a deep cape, for in the *Weekly Rehearsal* of April 10, 1732, a runaway slave is advertised as wearing off an "Orange colour'd Riding Hood with Armholes." In old embroideries and prints we see good examples of riding-hoods.

In 1724 Mr. Thomas Amory wrote to England for a "good fashionable fine riding-hood or a cloak with a hood to it embroidered. Any color would do except red or yellow." The following year, in Madam Usher's wardrobe were "Nine hoods of Several Sorts." Mistress Estabrook, wife of the parson at Windham, Conn., had many hoods of silk and gauze and serge and camlet.

In 1737 "Fine, cource, and Pug Hoods" were advertised by Boston milliners in Boston papers, and "Tossells for Hoods" also. "Pugs" were in fashion for many years. Velvet hoods, and gauze hoods appeared in season. Gypsy hoods, too, had their day. Then came muskmelon hoods and pumpkin hoods—the latter perhaps the hottest head-coverings ever invented outside an Esquimau igloo—a hood that, as Tom Brown said, "would make a Laplander sweat at the North Pole." These clumsy pumpkin hoods were made of great rolls of wool padding placed between double woollen covering, and held in place by quiltings or cords.

It would appear also that men wore some form of head-gear like a hood and also called a hood. Judge Sewall donned one, probably to protect his neck, since he wore no wig.

HOOPS. When Margaret Winthrop and Priscilla Molines landed on the unknown shore of New England, their clinging garments were not distended and disfigured by hoops. Nor do I find any signs of the reign of hoops or "vardingales" in New England until the eighteenth century, save in the will of one Elizabeth Cutler in 1663, where she mentions a "Morone coulour'd Carsey Houp" worth sixteen shillings. With the opening of the century, hoops came in fashion, for in 1701 Solomon Stoddard wrote to Judge Sewall, mentioning "hooped petticoats" as trenching on morality. Indeed the tradition assigned for their assumption seems to have put them in bad repute everywhere ever since 1596, when the author of *Pleasant Quippes for Upstart New-Fangled Gentlewomen* thus wrote:

> These hoops that hippes and haunch do hide
> And heave aloft the gay hoyst traine,
> As they are now in use for pride,
> So did they first beginne of paine.

But hoops were quickly tolerated, even by very godly Puritan folk, for when William

Pepperell married Judge Sewall's granddaughter, Mary Hirst, in 1723, one of the bridegroom's valued wedding gifts was a hooped petticoat; and I doubt not Mistress Mary Pepperell walked proudly to the North Church on the following Sabbath with dress spread out over her new hoop as she "came out bride" observed of all in the narrow Boston street and in the Puritan meeting-house.

In 1713 there was printed in Boston "A Satyr, in Verse: Origin of the Whalebone Petticoat," showing by the advent of caricacature that the reign of hoops had begun. The ban of religion was also placed on the unwelcome fashion. The *New England Courant* offered for three pence, in 1722, a little book "intituled"—"Hoop-Pettycoats Arraigned and Condemned by the Light of Nature and Laws of God." On April 19, 1728, "Womens Hoop Coats" were advertised in the *New England Weekly Journal*, and at the same time Mr. Amory, a rich Boston merchant, condemned and returned a lot of petticoats consigned to him from England, because they were too scanty for wear with the hoops then in vogue. In 1740 "Quilted and Hooped Petticoats" were imported, and petticoats suitable to large or small hoops. Hooped coats appeared,—"Long & Short Bone Hoop Coats," and "Hooping Holland;" the latter evidently to make strong linen petticoats into which reeds or bones could be run, as Pope said, "arm'd with ribs of whale." Whalebone and reeds were also plentifully sold, and cane and "quhaill-horne"—which was only another name for whalebone. The size and spread of hoops at this date may be fancied, when it is told that there were advertised in 1748, in the *Boston Independent Advertiser*, "Fine Newest Fashion Hoop Petticoats from 3 yards to 5 yards made with fine Long Bone." The shapes of hoops varied in New England, as in England and France. Fly hoops were worn in 1755. Jane Eustis, a fashionable Boston mantua-maker and shopkeeper, had "Fan Hoops" for sale in 1758. In 1721 came "Bell Hoops" of pyramidal shape, very large at the base; and "Pocket Hoops"—great panier-shaped humps, one on each hip—the ugliest and most cumbersome fashion ever in vogue, were worn in 1750 and also in 1780. The portrait of Juliana Penn, daughter-in-law of William Penn, shows pocket hoops standing out a foot and a half horizontally from the waist. In an old piece of tapestry embroidered in 1756, portraying a wedding procession in Boston, the women all wear pocket hoops. The portrait of Mrs. Nicholas Boylston (1765) displays a big hoop. The advertisement of children's hoops and hoop-coats proves that little girls ballooned through Boston, New York, and Philadelphia streets as universally and unbecomingly as did their modish mothers. The shapes of all these hoops followed closely those of England; swelling at the sides in vast "rumps" in Boston within a year after that ugly fashion obtained in London; standing out in a vast circle around the feet of the sensible wives of the Salem merchants and Charleston and Annapolis ship-owners, just as similar ones proudly surrounded the limbs of patrician English duchesses. The classic garb of the court of Josephine banished hoops for a time, only to return until our own day in constantly recurring waves of fashion.

HOSE. The words hose and stockings seem to have been, from earliest New England days, interchangeable. When doublet and hose were worn, the latter were of course the long Florentine hose, somewhat like our modern tights. In the list of goods furnished to the colonists in 1628, by the Massachusetts Bay Company, both are named. "300 peare of stockings w'of 200 pere Irish about 11^{d} or 13^{d} a p. 100 peare of knit stockings about 2^{s} 4^{d} a pr., 200 sutes dublett and hose of leather lyned w'th oil'd skyn Lether, ye hose & dublett with hookes and eyes. 100 sutes of Norden dussens or hampheere kersies lyned the hose with skyns." The Piscataquay planters had in 1635 "40 Doz Coarse Hose, 204 Pair Stockins, 149 Pair Small Hose," which were all, I think, stockings. I judge from the number of pair of breeches supplied to these Piscataquay settlers that long hose were in 1635 no longer in vogue.

Gayly colored stockings appear to have been worn. We find John Eliot ordering "greene & blew Cotton Stockings" in 1651. In 1667 a Hartford gentleman had sent to him from England a pair "Pinck colour'd mens hose" worth a pound, and a "paire of womens green hose worth thirteen shillings, and ten paire mens silke hose." Yellow stockings were ordered from England in 1660 for one who wished to appear irradiated like Malvolio. In 1739 russet and green were the favorite colors. By Revolutionary times white silk hose were worn by modish beaux.

Cloth stockings, such as Queen Elizabeth wore, are frequently named in lists. In 1675 eighteen dozen sold for £14 8s. The Irish stockings so often imported must have been of cloth or felting, for in *New England's First Fruits* we read instructions to bring over "good Irish stockings, which if they are good are much more serviceable than knit ones." There appears to have been much variety in shape, as well as in material. John Usher, writing in 1675 to England, says, "your sherrups stockings and your turn down stockings are not salable here." Judge Sewall orders in 1723, "two pair good Knit Worsted Stockings of the colour of the inclosed Cloth; not to roll, not Picked Snouts, but Round Toes. Two pair of good Mill'd Stockings of a dark Colour, round Toes." Roll-up stockings were worth 10 shillings a pair in 1691. "Indean Stockings" were bequeathed. They were probably leather leggins. Leather stockings were also worn, even by such a dignitary as William Penn.

Stirrup stockings and socks were advertised in the *Boston News Letter* of January 30, 1731. Stirrup-hose are described and drawn by Randle Holme in his note-book, dated 1658, which is preserved in the British Museum. They were very wide at the top—two yards wide—and edged with points or eyelet holes by which they were made fast to the girdle or bag-breeches. Sometimes they were allowed to bag down over the garter. They are said to have been worn on horseback to protect the other garments; but Holme speaks of other hose being worn over them.

"Diced Hose, masqueraded hose, silk cloked & chevered hose, Fine four-thread Strawbridge knit hose, yarn hose, ribbed pointed chivelled worsted hose, Jersey knit hose," all were sold in Boston previous to 1740, showing that "many dispositions of hose" were known.

HUM-HUM A plain coarse-meshed Indian fabric made of cotton, much advertised in the middle of the century. We read of "blue Humhums" and "Humphumps for Sacks" for sale in various Boston newspapers, from 1750 to 1770.

INKLE. A woollen tape or braid formerly used by simple folk as a trimming, being sewed on in patterns. Autolycus had inkles in his pack to sell to the shepherds. John Pyncheon charged thirteen pence for "a bunch of Incle" in his Springfield shop in 1651. Inkles were sometimes striped. I find them advertised till Revolutionary times in New England papers, in this wise: "Rich inkle lustring," "striped inkle," "stay inkle," etc. In England the name is now applied to a broad linen tape.

IZAVEES. Elizabeth Murray had "Izavees for Sacks" in 1752. This may have been a New England spelling of Vis-à-vis.

JACKET. Edward Skinner had a jacket in 1641; and after 1720 jackets seem to have been worn much by servants, for they appear in the inventories of the garb of runaways: a swanskin jacket in 1720; "dark almost black Double Breasted Frieze Jacket" in 1720; "Pee Double-Breasted Jacket with Brass Buttons" in 1730; and a "cinnamon-coulour'd Jacott" in 1733. Linen jackets were worn by southern slaves.

JERKIN. Strutt says that a jerkin, a jacket, and a coat were the same thing. In Meriton's *Clavis*, 1697, the compiler says a "jerkin is a kind of jacket or upper doublet with four skirts or laps." In *Two Gentlemen of Verona*, act 2, sc. 4, we read, "My jerkin is a doublet:" and both names appear to have been applied to the same garment, and also to a buff-coat. The name is not frequently seen in America, even in early colonial inventories. Edward Skinner of Boston had "1 Ircken" in 1641. Governor Winthrop had a "two tufted velvet jerkin." Maryland planters had erkyns. It was also spelt jorgen and jergen, and, as in old Dutch, jurkken. A jerkinet was a similar garment for women's wear.

JIMP. See JUMP.

JOSEPH. A name given in the eighteenth century to a lady's riding habit or great-coat buttoned down the front, and with a broad cape. It is said to have been named in allusion to Joseph's coat of many colors. We know that Olivia, in the *Vicar of Wakefield*, was to have her portrait painted "dressed in a green joseph."

A curious diminutive or degraded form of the word and garment was used in the Middle States. In the *New York Mercury* of June 16, 1760, we read of a runaway maid-servant wearing off "peniston Josey," and another a "blue and white Cotton Josey."

JORGEN. See JERKIN.

JUMP. "A loose stays or waistcoat" used in negligée dress. We read in the *Universal Magazine* of 1780:

> Now a shape in neat stays,
> Now a slattern in jumps.

And again, "Bless me, don't mind my shape this bout, I'm only in jumps." In November, 1754, in the *Boston Evening Post* "Womens and Maids stays and Jumps" appear; and also in New York papers of the same date. From the entries in early wills of the seventeenth century, it would seem that the word "jump" was then applied to waistscoats and bodices worn for outer garments, not to a loose stays worn as an undergarment. Randle Holme describes it as "a jacket, jump, or loose coat reaching to the thighs." Jumps were also called jimps and may have been derived from jupe. We read in Burns, "My ladies jimps and jerkinet." I think our word in modern use, jumper, a loose overall jacket, is derived from jump.

KERCHIEF. See HANDKERCHIEF.

KERSEY.

Be thine of Kersey firm though small the cost
Then brave unwet the Rain, unchill'd the Frost.

Kersey was a firm woollen cloth made of long-fibred wool, and was known in England as early as the time of Edward III. It was spelt in America in the usual ingenious assortment of ways, carsey being the favorite form. From it were made the garments of the Pilgrims on the Mayflower, those of the Massachusetts Puritans, the Virginian Cavaliers, and the Maine fishermen. In 1640 seven yards of kersey were worth £1 8*s*. By an inventory of one Leadlaw in Saco, Me., in 1662, we learn it was then and there worth ten shillings a yard. By 1692, settler Foxcroft, writing to England with regard to future importations to the new land, said, "Kerseys & Cource Linens are a Drug." Devonshire carsey is mentioned in early wills, and appeared in newspaper advertisements from 1704 until the latter part of the last century, especially in the description of the dress of runaways, in the *Boston News Letter* of September, 1704, as when an eloping servant wore "Gray homespun Devonshire Kersey breeches," and again, when an Indian maid wore off a "Kersey Peticote."

KHANTSLOPER. See SLOPS.

Kit-Packs. See Buskin.

Lace. The word lace was applied in early days both to a lacing cord and, as we now use it, to an open-work trimming lace. A lace was originally the cord that held garments in place, and as it was crossed backward and forward it formed open-work meshes, the prototype of the lace meshes. When Sir William Pepperell wrote abroad in 1737 for "A gold Lace for a Hat and Botten for my Selfe and a Lace for ye knees and a paire of Breeches," he meant probably gold cords.

In 1634 the Massachusetts General Court made many rigid laws forbidding the wearing of "any app'ell either wollen silke or lynnen with any lace on it, Silver, golde, silke or thread." These laws did not, however, work the desired end; many women and men were prosecuted and fined for wearing lace, "Ester wife of Joseph Jynkes Jr. of Lyn" being among the number. In Connecticut a similar law existed. "What person soever shall weare gold or silver lace or any bone lace above 3 sh a yard, shall be assessed at one hundred and fifty pounds estate."

Bone lace was used by the earliest colonists—the Pilgrims themselves and the Jamestown settlers, and also in England in the sixteenth century.

> The spinsters and the knitters in the sun
> And the free maids that weave their thread with
> bones.

Thus wrote Shakespeare in his *Twelfth Night.* Fuller in his *Worthies* says this lace was called bone lace because made with bone bobbins; and he defended its use because its material was not expensive, because its manufacture employed children and infirm persons, and because it saved the spending of many thousands of pounds yearly by Englishmen for lace in Flanders.

In the printed notice of the prize of a privateersman, in colonial days, we find "bone lace," and it was advertised for sale for many years in New England newspapers—in 1736 in the *New England Weekly Journal,* "Black Bone Lace;" and in 1749 in the *Boston Independent Adver-*

tiser. And it was used to trim gowns and smocks, and capes, and petticoats, as inventories show. And industrious New England maids, Judge Sewall's daughters among the number, were taught to make it on their lace cushions.

New England dames had imported laces also to choose from. The portraits of the times show many frills and collars of various laces. In 1712 "Gymp'r Lace" was imported, worth twelve shillings a yard. It was also called "Gimp Lace." "Dutch Lace, Blond Lace, Black Silk Lace" came next. In 1727 came "Fine Mechlon Silk Laces & Edgings;" while Magdalen Wroe had Machlin Lace. "Scarlet & Crimson Silk Lace with Mantle Tossels" were advertised in the *New England Weekly Journal* in 1736. Flanders lace came frequently, and snail laces. Campane lace, a very narrow pillow lace used as an edge, was, I suppose, campaign lace. It was made in gold and colored silk as well as in white. Blown lace was the commonest of all.

Colverteen, also spelt golbertaine, collertine, collertain, and colbertine, was a lace with square meshes, so called from Louis XIV.'s minister, Colbert, who promoted the lace industry. It was used to trim bands and caps. We read in Swift's *Baucis and Philemon* of "good pinners edged with colberteen." Curiously enough the name was not used in France. In 1755 Bath lace, Mechlin, "bonseel," Flanders, Brussels, minott, coxcomb, "traly," "taste," blond and bone laces were all imported. Traly or trolley lace was made in Devonshire. It had a double ground of hexagonal and triangular meshes. The pattern was outlined with a heavier thread. Minott, or minuet, or minuit, or mignonette lace was a narrow bobbin lace resembling tulle, or our modern footing; it was made chiefly at Arras and Lille. Five years later "thread inlet," "cheveau du friz" (which I think was fly-fringe) and "spider" laces were imported.

It is impossible to definitely describe these laces. Mrs. Bary-Palliser's book on laces gives some information. They were doubtless much like our hand-made laces of the present day; our blond, Mechlin, thread, and Brussels laces.

Gold and silver laces were worn by men, and occasionally lace-edged ruffles at the shirt front and wrists, and a few lace-edged cravats were seen in Virginia; but "true New England men" and Quakers followed no extreme cavalier fashions, nor did the Dutch. See NET.

LAPPET. The lace pendant of a lady's cap or head-dress. Horace Walpole called them "unmeaning pendants." In the *Boston Gazette* of November 13, 1750, we read of "Lappitt Heeds," and in the *Boston Evening Post* of September, 1758, Jane Eustis advertised "Blown Lace Lappet Heads." In 1772 came "Very Neat Flanders and Brussels Lappet Heads." In many of the portraits of the times we see long lace lappets on the caps.

LELLOKANS. See PINS.

LENO. A thin gauzy linen made in imitation of muslin, and much used for caps and head-dresses a hundred years ago.

LEVITE. Lady Cathcart—an American

by birth—writing to her aunt in 1781, gave thus the London fashions:

> They wear for morning a white poloneze or a dress they call a Levete, which is a kind of gown and Peticote with long sleeves made with scarcely any pique in the back, and worn with a sash tyed on the left side. They make these in winter of white dimity, and in Summer of Muslin with Chints borders.

This explains the advertisements in the *Boston Evening Post* of 1783, of "callicoes for Levites."

The levite was originally a long straight frock-coat somewhat like that worn by a priest. Horace Walpole satirized it as resembling "a man's nightgown tied round with a belt." The robe-levite imitated it with a train added. A "monkey-tailed levite" had a curiously twisted train, and was a French fashion. In the translation, by Mrs. Cashel Hoey, of Robida's *Ten Centuries of Toilette* there is shown on page 177 a levite robe—and a very modish-looking garment it is. The word Levite, like the robe, is now obsolete.

LILLIKINS. See PINS.

Liripipes. Pendent streamers to a hood or head-dress, often long enough to hang to the feet. These liripipes were of gauze or ribbons and were not used as strings, but were simply ornamental. Also spelt lyripups and lerrypups. The word was derived from *liripipium*, a hood of a particular form formerly worn by graduates. See Lappet.

Lockets. Michael Wigglesworth, author of the dreadful *Day of Doom* was a warm lover; he gave to his third wife, while he was wooing her, a dainty little heart-shaped locket, which is still owned by one of his descendants. Other colonists owned these pretty trinkets; John Oxenbridge had two. The widow of Colonel Livingstone, of New London, had a "stone drop for the neck and a red stone for a locket." "Stone heart lockets for hair sett in gold" were advertised in 1762, and "mocus lockets" and "silvered lockets." Lockets were worn on both the arm and the neck.

Loretto. A silk material much used for fine waistcoats in 1767.

Lustring. A soft plain silk universally worn. It was neither corded nor figured nor had it a satin surface. We find Judge Sewall, writing to England in 1697, for "forty yards of Flower'd Lustring not to exceed 5 sh per yard," for petticoats, and also for silk fringe to trim these lustring petticoats. Thomas Amory, writing to England in 1721, said "Lutstrings are staple commodities." The fashionable colors in lustrings in 1783 were, "Plumb, Pink, Flystale, Cinnamon, and Laylock," so said the *Newport Mercury*. The name appears till the middle of this century in common use.

Mandillion. A man's garment something of the nature of a doublet and also spelt mandilian. It was first worn in France in the sixteenth century, and was for many years a soldier's wear, and was frequently sleeveless. Chapman, in his translation of the *Iliad*, writes thus of a mandillion :—

About him a mandillion that did with buttons meet,
Of purple, large, and full of folds, curl'd with a warmful nap.

Mandillions were among the articles of clothing given to each Bay and Piscataquay planter.

The mandillions of the New England colonists were fastened with hooks and eyes, and lined with cotton.

MANTEAU. See MANTUA.

MANTELET. See MANTLE.

MANTO. See MANTUA.

MANTLE. In 1662 Mary Lake, of Ipswich, had a scarlet mantle appraised at £4. Penelope Winslow, the wife of the governor of Plymouth Plantations, had her portrait painted at about that date in a similar scarlet mantle. In the *New England Weekly Journal*, of 1739 we read of the sale of "Manteels," and in 1743, in the *Boston News Letter*, that "Ladies may have their Mantelets made." The words mantle and mantelet were closely akin to the word mantua, *q. v.*

MANTUA. Originally a gown or sacque open to display the petticoat; then the outer mantle or cape, and finally a stuff for the making of mantuas. So universal was the wear of mantuas that they gave their name to the maker of cloaks — a mantua-maker. Silks for mantues, manteaus, and mantuas appear in all the eighteenth century newspapers. In the *Boston News Letter* of April 5, 1729, we read of the setting-up of a milliner who "designed the making of Mantos and Riding Dresses." In 1741 came yellow mantua silk. In 1755 Elizabeth Murray had "Enamelled Mantuas" for sale.

MARCASITE. Marcasite, spelled also marcassite, marchasite, marquesett, or marquaset, was a mineral, the crystallized form of iron pyrites. It was largely used in the eighteenth century for various ornamental purposes, chiefly in the decoration of the person. It could be readily polished, and when cut in facets like a rose-diamond, formed a pretty material for shoe and knee buckles, ear-rings, rings, pins, and hair ornaments. Scarce a single advertisement of wares of milliner or mantua-maker can be found in eighteenth century newspapers, that does not contain (in some form of spelling) the word marcasite, and scarce a rich gown or head-dress was seen without some ornament of marcasite.

MASKS. For many years the fair colonists, Quakers, Huguenots, and Puritans, had a fashion of wearing "sun-expelling masks," to protect the complexion against the wind, sun, and cold. Children wore them also. George Washington sent abroad for masks for his wife and for his little step-daughter, "Miss Custis;" and "childrens masks" are often named in bills of sale. Loo-masks were small half masks and were also imported. Sometimes these masks were held in the hand; but riding masks were often fitted with a silver mouthpiece, by which the close-set lips or teeth of the wearer could hold the protecting mask in place, since her hands were otherwise occupied with the reins or holding herself on the pillion. Sometimes, following an old-time French fashion, the mask had fastened to the mouth-opening two short silken strings with a silver bead or button at the end of each. With a bead placed in either corner of her mouth, the mask wearer could talk and still hold her mask firmly in place. For a while it was fashionable to wear the mask or vizard hanging by a ribbon or cord at the side. In 1645 masks were forbidden to be worn in Plymouth, Mass., for "improper purposes," and I have puzzled long over what those improper purposes could have been in that staid, pious, and small community. In 1654 one Burril, of Lynn, mentioned two masks in his inventory of property. In the following year one dozen black velvet masks were inventoried as worth £1 4*s*. As early as 1685 New York dames had masks, and they were sent to the South Carolina settlers. In 1729 they were advertised for sale in Philadelphia. For many years all invoices of English goods exported to America contained masks. From 1760 to 1790 they were mentioned in almost every list of goods offered to New England shoppers, and must have been universally worn. They were of black velvet, white silk, green silk, and "natural coloured," which latter kind must have been specially disfiguring and ugly.

MATCH-COAT. The definition given two centuries ago by Governor Beverley of Virginia was this:

> The proper Indian matchcoat is made of skins dressed with the fur or sewed together. The Duffield matchcoat is bought of the English.

The name match-cloth was given to a coarse woollen cloth used for these coats, but duffels were chiefly employed in their manufacture. The derivation of the word seems uncertain. In Baroga's *Chippewa Dictionary* the word *matchigode* is given for petticoat.

MERCURY. A mercury was a cap or head-dress for women's wear, often mentioned in public sales. From the *Boston Evening Post*, of 1760 and 1761, we gain an idea of the materials used in these mercuries—gauze, net, trolly, beads, bugles, lace, etc.

MILLY. The name of a color which apparently was nearly meal-colored. I have often read of milly, tuly, and murry woollens being ordered.

MINIKINS. See PINS.

MITTENS. Wadmoll mittens were among the supplies furnished to the Bay planters. Knit mittens and those made of heavy cloth and fur were constantly worn. We read of runaways wearing off "jarning" and "yarn mittens." The knitting of mittens was for many years a lucrative household industry, and much ingenuity was displayed in the various ornamental stitches employed and pride in the short time employed in knitting. Many girls could knit a pair of double mittens in a day. Thrummed mittens were knit from the thrums of wool, and were much cheaper. Mittens were also made of heavy cloth, and of the skins of various animals.

MITTS. Little fingerless gloves were for many years much worn and went by the name of mitts. They were made of kid or silk and frequently of open lace-work, and were a favorite summer wear. We find them advertised in the *Boston Evening Post*, of November, 1750, of various gay colors—pink, blue, and yellow, which were probably for evening wear. I have seen old mitts of woven silk with handsome medallions of lace set in on the back of the hand. A curious kind of mitts was worn just after the Revolution. Fingerless covers, like sleeves, for the arms, with a short separate thumb covering, but no finger divisions, were made of cotton or linen material like the dress, and were freshly starched and ironed for Sunday wear. They were buttoned to the shoulder of the dress. Such mitts were often made of yellow nankeen to wear with a short-sleeved nankeen gown. I think the "Womens & girls Jane and Linen Mitts" and "White Holland Gloves," which were advertised in Boston in 1784, must have been these uncomfortable sleeve-mitts. And when the wife of Colonel John May, of Boston, wrote in her diary on June 5, 1789, "Cut my girls gloves, set them to work, and left them to take care of the house," the gloves named doubtless were these linen mitts.

MOB. See CAP.

MOCUS. Mocus, mocho, morko, or mochu was what is now known as moss-agate or dendritic agate. These "mocuses" were vastly modish in England in Queen Anne's day, set in rings, seals, brooches, buckles, and necklaces and were in high fashion in the colonies. I find them largely advertised in New York and Pennsylvania newspapers.

MODESTY-PIECE. Addison thus describes it: "A narrow lace which runs along the upper part of the stays before, being a part of the tucker, is called the modesty-piece." It was also called modesty-bit. See GORGET and STOMACHER.

MONMOUTH CAP. See CAP.

MUCKENDER. See HANDKERCHIEF.

MUFF. Muffs are said, by some English authorities, to have been introduced into England in the reign of Charles II. This is obviously incorrect, since Thomas Cullamore, of St. Marys, Maryland, had a muff in 1638, and Alice Ferrance of Boston left a "muffe" by will in 1656, and Jane Humphreys of Dorchester one with a winter hood in 1668. Judge Sewall bought, in England, muffs of Yarman Serge, and four other "good muffs" that he bought for his family —his wife and daughters—cost £2 6*s*. He also ordered muffs from abroad at later dates. Cloth as well as fur muffs were made. The *Connecticut Courant* had this startling advertisement. "Ladies will obtain muffs much cheaper by bringing their own skins." A few of the different materials that I have noted in advertisements are here named: "Martin Muffs & Tippits," "New Feather'd Muffs," "Swan feather'd muffs," "Blue & colored velvet muffs," "Mouse colour'd muffs of a peculiar kind;" which were apparently all for women's wear. Muffs grew to an enormous size and were carried for many years by both men and women. On March 5, 1715, the *Boston News Letter* contained this advertisement:

> Any man that took up a Mans Muff drop't on the Lords Day between the Old Meeting House & the South are desired to bring it to the Printers Office and shall be rewarded.

In 1725, Dr. Prince lost his "black bear-skin muff," and in 1740 a "sable-skin mans muff" was advertised. In this, as in other fashions, New England beaux followed the lead of English dandies. Many diaries and letters—such as those of Horace Walpole—show the prevalence of the fashion of "mans muffs" in England. I can easily fancy the mincing face of Horace Walpole peering out of a carriage window or a sedan chair, with his hands and wrists thrust in a great muff; but when I look at the severe and ascetic countenance in the portrait of Thomas Prince I find it hard to think of him, walking solemnly along Boston streets, carrying his big bear-skin muff. Other Bostonians followed the fashion until a much later date—Judge Dana until after Revolutionary times. In New York René Hett had several muffs which he left by will in 1783.

Muffetees. Muffetees were what we would now call wristlets, and were worn by men, and possibly by women. The sleeves of men's coats were made very short in order to display fine lace or lawn wrist ruffles. Hence the wrists were thinly clad and much exposed to the cold. Long gloves with gauntlets were worn for protection, and muffetees. These were of fur or woollen. In the *Boston Gazette and Weekly Journal* of November, 1749, "Men's fine Worsted Gloves and Muffetees" were offered for sale; and in the same paper, in 1755, "white black and colour'd Muffetees" were advertised. They were also knit of yarn.

MURRY. A reddish purple color—mulberry color. The livery colors of the house of York were murry and blue. I have often seen the word murry in lists of merchandise of early colonial days. It was a favorite color for the garments of respectable elderly gentlemen.

NABOBS. Eliza Southgate Bowne, writing in 1803 of the fashions, says "silk nabobs plaided, colored, and white, are much worn." In other letters of ten years earlier date we read of nabobs for women's wear, but with no definite descriptions thereof; and any such signification of the word is not given in our dictionaries. Nabobs were probably a thin East Indian stuff.

NANKEENS. Fairholt says nankeens were introduced into America, in 1825, from Sicily. His statement is absurdly incorrect, for I find them advertised for sale in the *Charleston Gazette* (S. C.) as early as May 7, 1744, and in 1761 in the *Boston Evening Post*, and read also of runaway slaves wearing nankeen breeches in 1769. George Washington bought them in large quantities as early as 1769. By 1780 they were a vastly important article of commerce in the India trade, and their price was almost a standard of exchange. They were used by all classes and both sexes for all variety of outer gear for both summer and winter wear, but must have proved rather chilly attire by Christmas-tide. The name is given from the place of manufacture, Nanking, in China, and the peculiar buff color is the natural tint of the cotton of which the nankeens are made.

NECK-CLOTH. Jane Humphreys, of Dorchester, Mass., owned in 1668, "A black sike (quilled) Neckcloath, a Black Stuffe Neck Cloath, and a Callico Vnder Neck

Cloath." Other colonists had speckled neck-cloths, lawn and silesia neck-cloths. Men and women both wore them. They were also called neck-clothes, neckerchiefs, neck-ingers, and neckatees.

NECKLACE. When the venerable Judge Sewall was courting Madam Winthrop for his third wife, he ingratiatingly asked her what kind of a "Neck-Lace" he should bring her, showing that these trinkets were then fashion-able and plentiful—and presumably low-priced (as were all the Judge's gifts), as well as proving them a true lover's token. In England, at the same date, Madam Pepys had "pitched upon a necklace with three rows of pearls which is a very good one, and so is the price." From early advertisements in the *Boston News Letter*, we learn some-thing of the fashion of the necklaces of those days. In June, 1712, a "White Stone fine-cut Necklace set in Silver" was lost—only two shillings reward was offered. In the *Boston Evening Post* of March 8, 1736, there was advertised "A spangled Gold Chain, three strings with a large Gold Locket having Abigail Andrews wrote upon it." £5 reward was offered for their recovery. In New York richer necklaces were worn, single and triple strings of pearls.

In 1753 we find "French and Solitair Necklaces," "light blue pendalls and Necklaces," "Pink and White Pearl colored Necklaces;" and by 1761 "Purple, green and black necklaces with spreaders." The latter must have been uncommonly ugly and were probably made of beads or bugles, and formed an *esclavage* or festooned necklace—a French fashion introduced in 1760. In 1771, J. Coolidge, Jr., had for sale in Boston "Necklaces, sprigs, solitairs and pends set with marquasetts." Many early portraits show necklaces, usually simple strings of beads, the latter frequently of gold. Many New England wives at a later date placed their hard-earned savings, their "egg and yarn money," in the portable, safe and easily salable shape of gold beads. In the diary of Abigail Kellond, kept from 1685 to 1730, she frequently enters the number of "goold beeds" on her and her daughter's necklaces. The latter had fifty-two in 1686, and thirty years later she had ninety-nine beads. Madam Kellond herself had one hundred and four beads.

NECKSTOCK.

> The stock with buckle made of paste
> Has put the cravat out of date,

wrote Whyte in 1742. The stock, a made-up, stiffly folded cravat or neck-cloth, with a metal spring attached to keep it in place when on the neck, is not wholly obsolete at the present day, though wholly old-fashioned and bucolic.

In 1743, in the *Boston News Letter*, two neck-stocks were advertised as lost; and in 1764 in the *Boston Evening Post* we find mention of "Stock-Tapes" and "Newest fashion'd plaited Stocks." In the *Connecticut Courant*, of May 1, 1773, and in New York journals we find silver plated and pinchbeck stock buckles "cypher'd and plain." These buckles were originally set as an ornament in the front of the stock, but in later days the stock was fastened on one side by a strong unornamented buckle, or by two small buckles and straps.

NEGLIGEE. A loose, full gown, open in front, which Fairholt says was introduced about 1757. I find in the *Boston Evening Post* of November, 1755, "Horsehair Quilted Coats to wear with Negligees," and they must have been fashionable at an earlier date in England than Fairholt stated. A poem printed in New York in 1756 has these lines:

Put on her a Shepherdee
A short sack or Negligee
Ruffled high to keep her warm
Eight or ten about an arm.

In spite of the signification of the name, a negligee was worn in full dress. Abigail Adams, writing to Mrs. Storer in 1785, said: "Trimming is reserved for full dress only, when very large hoops and negligees with trains three yards long are worn." We find Benjamin Franklin sending home materials for negligees for his Deborah in 1765.

NET. Though we still have various machine-made nets, we have no such variety as were advertised a century ago, and which seem to have been frequently a fine gauze, rather than an open-meshed net. Some of the curious names were: picket or piquet net, whip-net, male or meal net, drop-net, spider net, balloon-net, warp-net, point-net, Paris net, bobbin-net, dress-net, undress-net, patent or pattern net, lace-net, dressed net, queens net, queens fancy net, caul-net. All these were used in the manufacture of caps, scarfs, and head-dresses, and for furbelows for gowns—some of them for the entire gown. See LACE.

NIGHTCAP. Everyone—men, women, and children — wore nightcaps as part of the sleeping attire, until modern times. When the Governor of Acadia sent to the government of Massachusetts the list of goods stolen from him by "Mr. Phips" he named "4 nightcaps with lace edge; 8 nightcaps without lace." Men at one time wore nightcaps in day-time as part of a negligée costume. I have seen ancient colored silk nightcaps richly embroidered in colors and gold and silver.

NIGHT-GOWN. The early signification of the word night-gown was much the meaning applied at present to the word dressing-gown. It was not a garment worn when sleeping. We have a very good description of a night-gown from the pen of the old Duchess of Marlborough, who ordered such a garment from Paris :

> A Night-gown easy and warm, with a light silk wadd in it, such as are used to come out of bed and gird round, without any train at all, but very full. Tis no matter what color, except pink or yellow—no gold or silver in it ; but some pretty striped satin or damask, lined with a tafetty of the same color.

When Madam Usher died in Boston in 1725, her wardrobe was sent to her daughter in London. It contained one satin and one silk night-gown, but the night rails were of linen. Men had velvet night-gowns with caps to match of the same material, and fustian night-gowns also. In the *Boston Evening Post,* in 1760, " Men's velvet Night gown Caps " are advertised. In 1754 a law was passed by the Corporation of Harvard College that no student should " wear any silk night-gowns as being not only an unnecessary expense but inconsistent with the gravity and demeanor proper to be observed." A letter written to the *New England Weekly Journal,* in 1727, speaks of a merchant sitting "in his Counting-house wrap't up in a Callimanco Night-gown." See RAIL.

NONE-SO-PRETTYS. About the year 1770 there began to appear in all the New England newspapers advertisements of "None-so-Prettys." The name was in the motley list which was characteristic of the times, and which gave no clew to the character of the articles offered; hence "None-so-Prettys" might be ladies' caps, or snuff-boxes, or tailors' goods. Nor do American or English dictionaries even now define the word. But William Scott, of the Irish linen store in Boston, advertised in July, 1771, "None-so-Pretty Tapes," and in September, 1772, the *Boston Evening Post* contained a notice of the sale of "Blue & white, Red & white, Green & white Furniture checks with None-so-Prettys to match;" so it is plain that None-so-Prettys were tapes. In a little story and a half brick shop in Wickford, R. I., which retained, until 1886, all the goods and ways of a village shop of the early part of the century, there was displayed, among boxes of half-melted, coherent red wafers, sheets of fly-specked foolscap paper, strings of purple and white beads, cakes of adamantine beeswax, brass tailors' thimbles, sailors' "palms," and other relics of past decades, a box labelled "None-so-Prettys." These were rolls of strong brown linen braid about three-quarters of an inch wide, with little woven figures, white, red, or black dots or diamonds. And from their faded, aged appearance, these None-so-Pretty survivors might well have been centenarians from the original stock of William Scott in 1771.

OZNABURG. A linen spelled ozenbridge, ossenbrigs, osnabrug, originally made at Osnabrück, Hanover, and universally used for shirts, breeches, and jackets. In the *Boston News Letter* of June 19, 1704, we read of a runaway slave's wearing off "Brown Ozenbridge Jacket and Breeches." A large item of value in Sir William Pepperell's orders to England were "peeces of Ossenbrigs." In the *Connecticut Courant* of December 11, 1775, Mary Jehonet advertised "Oznabrigs" for sale. To the Southern colonies it was sent in vast bales, and was used for garments for the slaves. We often find George Washington writing for "ozenbrigs."

ORRICE. A kind of lace or gimp trimming woven with gold and silver thread. It was widely used in the seventeenth century as a trimming for handsome sacques and petticoats. The name was applied at a later date to upholstery gimps, especially for those used for saddle trimmings.

PADUASOY. A rich silk of smooth surface, originally made at Padua. "The Best Sort Dutch Paduasoys" were advertised in the *Boston News Letter* in 1727, and in other newspapers till the end of the century. It was much used for handsome garments for men and women. We find Governor Belcher writing in 1732 to his London tailor, "One suit to be a very good silk. I have sometimes thought a rich damask would do well, or some thick silk, but I don't like padisway."

Paragon. A stuff, plain or embroidered, used for common wear in the seventeenth century. Madam Pepys had a paragon petticoat in 1659. One of the colonists left a "paragon coat," and one of the Salem witches wore a "red paragon bodice." It was the wear of country folk. We read,

> Give me a lass that's country bred
> With paragon gown; straw hat on her head.

Partlet. A sort of neckerchief or neck-covering for women's wear, which sometimes was made full like a shirt and worn under a bodice. The edge around the throat was frequently plaited or ruffled. We read in Beaumont and Fletcher's *Knight of Malta*,

> Unfledge 'em of their tires,
> Their wires, their partlets, pins and periwigs.

The name is seen but rarely in early colonial inventories.

Patches. In the *Boston Gazette and Weekly Journal*, of 1775, "Gum Patches" were advertised, and after 1760 "Face Patches" and "Patches for Ladies" appear with such frequency that we can believe patched faces were as common among Boston, New York, and Philadelphia belles, as with fashionable London court dames. Whitefield wrote bitterly and indignantly of the jewels, patches, and gay apparel worn by New England women. Still I have seen no portraits of New Englanders wearing patches.

Patch Box. With all the advertisements of face patches, there could not fail to be notices of the sale of patch boxes. The earliest appears in the *Boston Evening Post* of July 17, 1763. A few of these patch boxes have been preserved to us—oval or round boxes about an inch and a half or two inches in diameter—pretty little trinkets of Battersea enamel on brass, or of china medallions set in silver gilt, or of tortoise shell and silver; always with a tiny mirror or disk of polished steel set within the lid, that in it the fair and vain owner might peep to place or rearrange her becoming patches. Frequently they bear on the top little posies:

"For Beauty's Face," "To the Fairest of her Sex," "When Virtue joins, Fair Beauty shines." One I have has the sensible advice, "Have Communion with Few, Be Familiar with One, Deal Justly with All, Speak Evil of None." Another thus reproves, "Vanity's a Vice—a foe to Virtue."

Sometimes they have the likeness of a mincing French beauty or a scene with a tiny shepherdess, or a little design of dots and rings, or festoons, and a basket of flowers, or two hearts with a connecting arrow, but more frequently a verse or posy. These patch boxes are among the daintiest relics of olden times.

Patten.

The Patten now supports each frugal Dame
That from the blue-eyed Patty takes the name.
—*Trivia.*

Fairholt says that modern pattens date their origin to the time of Queen Anne. I find Sewall, in the time of William and Mary, referring to his wife's slipping and falling, through her being on pattens; and Ben Jonson says, "You make no more haste than a beggar upon pattens."

Pattens were iron rings four or five inches in diameter supporting, by two or three attached uprights, a sole of wood to be fastened to the foot by leather straps.

Though Dickens speaks in *David Copperfield* of "women going clicking about in pattens," and in *Cranford* we read of their wear, in New England they certainly were not frequently worn in this century and I have never found a pair of pattens in any old New England home. In the *Boston News Letters*, of 1721 and 1732, "womens and childrens pattoons" were often advertised, and similar notices appear in the newspapers until Revolutionary times. See CLOGS and GOLOSHOES.

PEAK. From the connection with surrounding items in advertisements, peaks would appear to be pointed caps for children's wear; but no such definition is assigned in any dictionary. This is hardly a safe inference to draw from the notices in colonial papers, for most heterogeneous and incongruous elements go to form a whole; and peaks might be toys or books or gowns or shoes. In 1737, Sept. 29, in the *New England Weekly Journal* appeared, "Children's Quilted Peaks drawn & work'd;" in the *Boston News Letter* in 1736, "Children's Silver Peaks & Flowers, Dutch Prettys;" and in 1740 a similar advertisement.

Pelerine. The derivation given is from *pèlerin*, a pilgrim. It seems much more probable that it is from *pelured*, meaning befurred. It was a lady's small cape with long ends hanging in front, and was invented to cover the necks bared by the low-cut French bodices. In 1743, in the *Boston News Letter*, Henrietta Maria East advertised that "Ladies may have their Pellerines made" at her mantua-making shop. In 1749 "pellerines" were advertised for sale in the *Boston Gazette* and a black velvet "pillerine" was lost. In the New York papers it was usually spelt pillareen. They are said to have been invented in 1671 in France by the Princess Palatine.

Penistone. This was spelt pennystone, peneston, penystones, penstow, penesstons, penston, and the goods were also called "Forest Whites." It was a coarse woollen stuff or frieze made in England in the seventeenth and eighteenth centuries and was much used for coarse garments by the earliest planters. Anne Leverett, of Boston, who died in 1656, bequeathed a "Read pennisto petticoat" to her heirs. In 1659 another Boston dame bequeathed to each of her grandchildren forty shillings "in kersey peniston and cotton." Hull, writing abroad in 1672, asks for "red penystone and flannel, no such red cloth as you sent me." I find the name used till 1780 especially in the South, and very frequently specified as red, and at other times evidently applied to red flannel.

PERIWIG. See WIG.

PERPETUANA. More frequently spelt "ppetuna." A glossy woollen stuff deriving its name, like sempiternum and lasting, from its alleged durable nature. It much resembled the latter named fabric. Bradford in his *Plymouth Plantation* wrote, "They had diverse kinds as cloth perpetuanes and other stuffs." We find, by a letter of Governor Endicott's, that twelve yards of red ppetuna were worth sixteen shillings in 1629. In the *Boston News Letter* of October 12, 1711, "Perpets" were advertised, which were also perpetuana.

PERSIAN. A thin silk chiefly used for cloak and hood linings, and for facings for other garments, or for summer wear. In 1737 Sir William Pepperell ordered from England several "ps Blue and Red Persian." It was offered for sale in New England newspapers throughout the eighteenth century. The only mention made by Judge Sewall of his wife's attire is when he speaks of her attending church, clad in her "gown of Sprig'd Persian."

PERUKE. See WIG.

PETTICOAT. This word was originally petty-coat, literally a small coat. In a tailor's bill are these items:

> To new plaiting a petty Coat, 1*s*. 6*d*.
> " sewing " " " 6*s*.

Judge Sewall wrote it "Petit Coats."

Of course this world-wide worn garment was donned in earliest colonial days, and the name appears in every list and inventory of feminine belongings. "Red Tamminy and Moehaire petticotes" had Martha Emmons of Boston, in 1666. Susannah Oxenbridge, wife of the wealthy Boston minister, had them of richer material — "changeable silke," "Finest tufted Holland," and "Blacke Cloth." Elizabeth Gedney had no less than thirteen petticoats; and Dutch dames counted their petticoats their richest belonging. I have seen the inventory of one Dutch woman's wardrobe that contained sixteen petticoats.

Quilted silk petticoats appeared for sale about 1720. "Women's Sarsnet Quilted Patticoats 4 yards wide, Persian and Taminy Ditto." "Long & Short Bone Hoop petticoats" are advertised in the *Boston Evening Post* of 1753.

Of course when the open sacques, negligées and poloneses were so much worn, and the petticoat was consequently so exposed to view, it became a most important and costly article of attire, was furbelowed, fringed, festooned, puffed, looped, rosetted, flowered, laced, and quilted in a hundred different fashions, and was made of every rich material.

PHILOMOT. See FILOMOT.

PILGRIM. A cape or plaiting of thin silk affixed to the back of a bonnet to shield the wearer's neck when out of doors. It was in use from 1760 to 1770.

PINCUSHION. Many newspapers contain notices of the sale of "pincushion hoops and chains." Usually they are printed in company with those of etuis or equipages, and I hence infer that ladies wore these swinging pincushions at their sides as a part of their chatelaines. These chains were of steel and silver. Dutch housewives constantly wore them.

PINS. The Pilgrim mothers brought over pins in the Mayflower, but not in lavish numbers. I find at a very early date that a woman was excommunicated for "suspitions of stealing pinnes;" and in 1643 "Will Fancies wife" was tried in New Haven for stealing five thousand pins. Pins were worth at that time 1*s.* 4*d.* a thousand. We know, too, what important instruments they proved in the tragedy known as the Salem Witchcraft. Henry M. Brooks, Esq., of the Essex Institute in Salem, has made a collection of pins taken from old documents and letters of past centuries. He has some which date positively to within a few years of the time of Salem witches, and may be quite as old as Ann Putnam's and Giles Corey's day. "Pinns" were sent to John Eliot by the Corporation in England in 1651. In the *Boston News Letter* of October, 1711, pins were advertised for sale. In the same publication of May 6, 1717, appeared this advertisement of what was apparently a Boston pinmaker, "All sorts of Pins also Black Pins for Mourning Either by Wholesale or Retail. Brass Wire Large & Small. Also any Person that has brass wire may have money for it." In 1737 Sir William Pepperell sent to England for "40 shillings in Pinnes of Different Sizes." In 1738 Ebenezer Waldo advertised that he "made and sold choice Pins of all Sorts for ready money at lowest prices." In 1744 they came "assorted in small boxes," and though "papers of pins of two sorts" were named, these were only loose pins wrapped in papers, not stuck in rows in paper as we buy them now. By 1775 pins began to have names—"Pins No. 4 & 12," "Durnford Pins;" and Harriot Paine at the Sign of the Buck and Glove had "corkins, middlings, short whites, lillikins, and lace pins." Others had Lellicins and Lellokans, which were all, I fancy, Mrs. Paine's lillikins, and Pound Pins and Pocket Brass Pins. In June, 1783, appeared in the *Boston Evening Post* the notice of Sheet Pins, which were, I suppose, sold stuck in sheets like our modern pins. We find George Washington ordering pins from England, "minikins," which were the smallest size, and were also called minifers.

PINNERS. This word has two meanings. The earlier use was precisely that of pinafore, or pincurtle, or pincloth—a child's apron. Thus we read in the Harvard College records, of the expenses of the year 1677, of "linnen Cloth for Table Pinners," which makes us suspect that Harvard students of that day had to wear bibs at commons. The second meaning was usually, when used in the plural, a woman's head-dress having long tabs or lappets that hung down the sides of the cheeks. We find Governor Berkeley of Virginia ordering, in 1660, "1 Yard of fine Lace for a piner," which was to cost £1 10*s*. In the *Boston News Letter* of August, 1728, a runaway slave-woman was advertised as wearing off a "suit of Plain Pinners," which was probably a cap or head-dress without the streamers or lappets. In 1737 the same paper advertised "Pinners or Dresses Just Arrived from London & Set in the Pink of the Mode."

Plaster Box. A box in which medicinal plasters were carried. It not only formed part of the outfit of physicians, but was an ornamental trinket in the dressing-case of gentlemen. Thus Isaac Addington, of Boston, who died in 1713, enumerated "my plaister-box" among his silver.

PLUSH. In 1695 Susannah Oxenbridge left a "Plush Gowne" to her parson's wife. Plush was advertised in the *Boston News Letter* of October 22, 1711, and of June 3, 1740—both silk and "hair and worsted" plushes.

POCKETS.

"Lost a Pocket with a worked Handkerchief, part of the Muslin was cut off & the Lawn begun to be sewed to the Work. There was a green Purse with about Five Pounds of Silver in it which the Finder is very welcome to if he will bring the Handkerchief to the Printer."

These pockets were ornamental bags, which were fastened on the outside of the gown. On them the fair wearer spent much time and skill. Elaborate designs in cross-stitch on canvas, bead and bugle work on velvet, are shown on these old pockets. The old song, "Lucy Locket lost her pocket," becomes easily comprehensible when we see these old-fashioned bags of pockets, which were wholly detached from the gown.

They were apparently sometimes made in pairs; as several "pairs of pockets" formed part of Madam Usher's wardrobe.

POINTS. Points were ties or laces of ribbon, or woollen yarn, or leather, decorated with tags, or aiglets at one end. They were employed instead of buttons in securing clothes, and were used only by the earliest settlers, and in New England, I think, solely as ornaments at the knee or for holding up the stockings. They were there regarded as but foolish vanities, and were one of the articles of finery tabooed in early sumptuary laws. In 1651 the General Court of Massachusetts expressed its "utter detestation and dislike that men of meane condition, education and calling should take upon them the garbe of gentlemen by the wearinge of poynts at the knees." We learn from the accounts of John Pyncheon in 1653 that "3 yds. garty points" were worth sixpence. These must have been cotton points. In the southern colonies silken points were worn. Justinian Snow, of St. Marys, Md., bought, in 1639, twenty-four dozen silk points worth nine shillings a dozen. These were probably of rich ribbon.

POLONESE. Fairholt says it was "a light

open gown which came into fashion about 1770 and was worn looped at the sides and trailing behind." This date must be entirely wrong. In November, 1755, "Cardinals & Polonees" were advertised in the *Boston Evening Post.* In September, 1756, in the same paper, "Figured Satin Dauphiness Cloaks & Polonese & Capuchins;" and in 1758, "Collored Pullanees." Of course they must have been worn in England much earlier than in the New World. The garment is said to have been so called from a Polish article of dress, and has at varying intervals been in vogue up to the present day.

We can gain some idea of the shape of an early polonese from the pages of the English *Lady's Magazine.* In 1774 it announced that

> Lady Tufnell has the genteelest fancy in an undress now in London. She chiefly wears a white Persian gown and coat made of Irish polonese and covered with white or painted spotted gauze which is very much the taste. The Irish polonese is made very becoming; it buttons half down the arm, no ruffles, quite straight in the back, and buttons down before and flies off behind, till there is nothing but a kind of role behind except the petticoat; a large

hood behind the neck; short black and white laced aprons or painted gauze.

It was also asserted in the same periodical, in 1776, that the Italian polonese was "much the most smart and becoming."

POMANDER. A pomander was derivatively a little ornamental pouncet-box of metal—usually silver, pierced with holes. In it was placed a ball of spices and scents. Through the holes the sweet perfume escaped. The pomander was sometimes swung at the side, but more frequently carried in the hand. The word pomander was originally applied to the spice-ball, and not to its inclosing box. The composition of a pomander was thus given: "Your only way to make a good pomander is this: Take an ounce of the purest garden mould cleans'd & steeped seven days in change of motherless rose water, then take the best labdanum, benjoin, both storaxes, ambergris, civit & musk. Incorporate them together and work them into what form you please."

POMPON. The *London Magazine*, of 1748, described a "pong-pong" (which was a pompon) as " the ornament worn by the ladies in the middle of the forepart of their headdresses. Their figures, size, and compositions are various, such as butterflies, feathers, tinsel, cockcomb, lace, &c." In a poem of same date I find this line, " A flower vulg. dict, a pompoon." In 1752 Elizabeth Murray had "pompeons" for sale in Boston. In November, 1755, in a rich invoice of fashionable novelties, came " Chinese pampoons," and a little later " pomparoons ; " so New England dames were not one whit behind English ones in the wear of the article, though possibly a little so in the spelling of it. Pompons were worn in Virginia and South Carolina.

PRUNELLA. A stuff like lasting. Governor Endicott, of Salem, left prunella by will in 1663. Susannah Oxenbridge, who died in Boston in 1695, left a "Blacke Prunella Gowne and Petticoat."

By 1740 it was largely used for the manufacture of women's shoes, and in 1772 we find " Strong rich black silk and Hair Prunella for Clergymens Coats and Waistcoats," and to women's shoes and clergymen's waistcoats and gowns it has since been relegated.

PUMPS. New England dandies wore, as did Monsieur À-la-mode:

> A pair of smart pumps made up of grain'd leather,
> So thin he cant venture to tread on a feather.

And not dandies only, but servants. A runaway negro slave was advertised in the *Boston News Letter* of 1726 as wearing off a "Pair of Pumps with Silver Buckles;" and Indians had "Peaked To'd Turn'd Pumps with white metal Buckles." Governor Belcher's negro Juba ran off shod in "a pair of trimmed Pumps with a very large pair of Flowered Buckles." If these pumps were as thin-soled as modern pumps, the wearers could not have run far. Women also wore pumps, made of morocco, lasting, and prunella; some pumps were double-channelled and turned; and children's pumps came to Boston and Hartford markets.

PURL. A species of edging for ruffs, ruffles, cuffs, etc. Mrs. Palliser says it is difficult to exactly define the difference between lace and purl. We read of "fine purle to set on a pinner." Wait Winthrop sent several times pieces of purle to his nieces at New London about the year 1690.

QUALITIES. A coarse binding tape advertised in the *Virginia Gazette*, the *Charleston Gazette*, and New England papers in the eighteenth century. The name is still in use.

QUEEN'S NIGHTCAP. See CAP.

QUEUE. Elizabeth Cutter had, in 1663, "six neck-clothes and six quieues" worth four shillings. Jane Humphrey, in 1668, named together "one of my best neckcloths and one of my plain quieues." These were evidently not the cues or wigtails of the succeeding century, but were a neck covering. I do not find the name, in the latter signification, in use after 1680.

QUIFE. See COIF.

QUOIFE. See COIF.

RABATO. Also spelt rebato and rebatine. A falling collar or band turned over upon the shoulders. "Stiff-necked rebatoes that have arches for pride to row under." The word was apparently used to distinguish any turned-down collar from a standing ruff, and was rarely used in America.

RAIL. The fashion of wearing "immoderate great rayles" was prohibited by law in Massachusetts in 1634. The garment at that date must have been a woman's loose gown or sacque worn in the daytime, for we cannot imagine even the meddlesome Massachusetts magistrates would dare to attempt to order what kind of a nightgown a woman should wear. But the name quickly was applied to a night garment. We read in a Boston newspaper of the loss of a "flowered callico nightrail with high collared neck;" and in inventories where cloth and velvet nightgowns appear, the rails are of linen and calico, thus proving it a garment worn when sleeping. I have seen the words bed-coat, and bed-gown, and bed-waistcoat used instead of nightrail. See NIGHTGOWN.

RAMILIES. See WIG.

RANELAGH MOB. See CAP.

RASH. A loose-meshed silk or wool stuff of inferior quality. We find one colonist complaining that, having sent to England for fine Spanish broadcloths at 17 shillings a yard, he was sent nothing but cloth rash worth 9 shillings a yard; and another wrote, in 1698: "Black Rashes are not Vendable here." In 1655 Robert Daniell, of Cambridge, Mass., had a "black Sut of Rash" worth a pound. It was evidently a stuff of smooth surface, for Donne, in his "*Satires*," wrote:

> Sleeveless his jerkin was, and it had been
> Velvet, but 'twas now (so much ground was seen)
> Become Tufftaffaty; and our children shall
> See it plain Rash awhile, then nought at all.

RATTEEN. A heavy stuff resembling drugget, advertised in March, 1748, in the *Boston Independent Advertiser*. Rattinet, also frequently imported, was a similar stuff, somewhat thinner.

RAYL. See RAIL.

Rebatine. See Rabato.

Ribbon. "Silken ribens" were of enough account in early days to be left by will, and denounced among superfluities by the Connecticut magistrates. They were a favorite gift on St. Valentine's Day. Among the ribbons advertised in the middle of the eighteenth century were paduasoy ribbons, love ribbons, Dettingen ribbons, Prussian ribbons, silvered ribbons, and in 1767, in the *Newport Mercury*, liberty ribbons.

Riding petticoat. See Safeguard.

Ring. Finger-rings were not rare at the date of the settlement of the New World, and the early colonists, who were men of dignity and position, nearly all possessed them, as did all well-to-do and dignified Englishmen. In the earliest colonial wills of the seventeenth century that have been preserved to us in court records and in private depositories we find frequent mention of them—usually, however, mourning rings.

Rings were given at funerals, especially in wealthy families, to relatives and to persons of note, wealth, or public office in the community. Sewall records in his diary, in the years from 1687 to 1725, the gift of no less than fifty-seven mourning rings. The story is told of Doctor Samuel Buxton, of Salem, Mass.,—who died in 1758, aged eighty-one years,—that he left to his heirs a quart tankard full of mourning rings which he had received at funerals. At one Boston funeral, in 1738, over two hundred rings were given away. At Waitstill Winthrop's funeral sixty rings, worth over a pound apiece, were given to his relatives and friends. Often fifty or a hundred rings would be given at a minister's or domine's funeral.

These mourning rings were of gold, usually enamelled in black. They were frequently decorated with a death's-head or a coffin with a skeleton lying in it, or a winged skull. Often they held a framed lock of hair of the deceased friend. Sometimes the ring was shaped like a serpent with his tail in his mouth. Many bore a posy. In the *Boston News Letter*, of October 30, 1742, was advertised: "Mourning Ring lost with the Posy Virtue & Love is From Above."

A favorite motto was: "Death parts United Hearts." Others bore the legend: "Prepare for Death;" another, "Prepared be to follow me." Some funeral rings bore a family crest in black enamel.

Goldsmiths kept these mourning rings constantly on hand. "Deaths Heads Rings" and "Burying Rings" appear in many newspaper advertisements. The name or initials of the dead person and the date of his death were engraved upon the ring to order. This was called fashioning.

It is very evident that the colonists looked with much eagerness to receiving a funeral ring at the death of a friend; and in old diaries, almanacs, and note-books such entries as this are often seen: "Made a ring at the funeral," "A Death's-head ring made at the funeral of" so and so. The will of Abigal Ropes, in 1775, gives to her grandson "a gold ring I made at his father's death;" and again, "a gold ring made when my bro. died."

I do not know how long the custom of giving funeral rings obtained in America. Some are in existence dated 1812, but were given at the funeral of aged persons, who may have left orders to their descendants to cling to the fashion of their youth.

A very good collection of mourning rings may be seen at the rooms of the Essex Institute, in Salem, and that society has also published a pamphlet, written by Mr. Curwin, giving a list of mourning rings known to be in existence in Salem.

Wedding rings were seldom named in New England inventories. Jane Humphreys, of Dorchester, Mass., had one in 1667. Mather said the Puritans made no use of rings at weddings; and one writer said they thought rings "a Relique of Popery and a Diabollicall Circle for the Divell to daunce in."

Robert Keayne, a wealthy citizen of Boston, was an early owner of what was called a "stoned ring." He left, in 1653, a "Great Gold Emerod Ring," which seems to still shed, with its great capital letters, a richly glittering green light. Other colonists had handsome rings; Parson John Wilson left, in 1688, a "gold ring with seal & an Enamelled ring." Governor Endicott's portrait has a handsome ring on the little finger. A ring presented to a member of the Winthrop family by Charles I. played an important part in history when re-presented to Charles II. by a New England Winthrop. Major John Pyncheon, of Springfield, Mass., had "6 gold rings and 1 Rubie ring." Mrs. De Lange, of New York, had two great diamond rings. Governor Caleb Carr, of Providence, R. I., named in his will in 1693, "Three gold Rings, my Seal ring and the gold ring I now weare commonly called hand in hand & heart between." The latter form of ring was fashionable for many years. I have often seen references to "heart and hand rings."

Parson John Oxenbridge died in Boston in 1673. Though he bemoaned his straitened circumstances, he owned and bequeathed "2 Carnelian Rings, 1 Ring beset with Blew Specks. [To his daughter Theodorah, who married Parson Thatcher.] My gold Ring with her name in it. My green Emeraud Ring with Diamond Sparks, and a Diamond Ring." He also left "A White Amethyst Ring. A Dozen Mourning Rings.

A Seale Ringe." All these save the latter were left to his daughters; but his widow, Susannah, must have had a pretty store of her own; for at her decease in 1695, she left a ring to nearly every minister in Boston. "My diamond ring" to Mr. Allen, and a gold ring to his wife; a ring to Joshua Moody; an emerald ring and gold ring to still another parson — ten rings in all. When Judith Sewall was betrothed, her lover gave her a "stoned ring, a fan and a noble letter," yet I find no definite notices of a fixed fashion of "betrothal rings." Cotton Mather was given a ring by the University of Glasgow, bearing the legend, "Glascua rigavit;" and Judge Sewall made frequent gifts of rings to friends, always with appropriate Latin mottoes.

As years passed on, advertisements appeared in the newspapers of rings lost, rings found, rings for sale. "Fine diamond rings, stoned rings, fashionable heart rings, carnelian rings, and mocus rings."

In the estate of one Jacobs, which was confiscated by a witch-hunting Salem sheriff in 1692, was "one Large Goold Thumb Ring worth twenty shillings ;" and in 1729 the *New England Weekly Journal* advertised a large thumb-ring picked up in Rumney Marsh.

Robings. Round robins or robings were narrow ruffs about the collar or neck of the gown. I find them usually offered for sale with cuffs and frequently also with stomachers. In 1751, in the *Boston Evening Post*, were named "a Variety of Robins & Cuffins fer Gowns." By June, 1753, Harriot Paine had "Snail Bugle & Silver Facings & Robings for the Ladies" for sale. Then came "Bugle Cuffings Robings & Stomachers."

Rocket. I think no better description of a rocket can be given than that of Celia Fiennes :—

> You meete all sorts of countrywomen wrapped up in the mantles called West Country Rockets, a large mantle doubled together, of a sort of serge, some are linsey-woolsey and a deep fringe or fag at the lower end ; these hang down, some to their feet, some only just below the waist ; in the summer they are all in white garments of this sort, in the winter they are in red ones.

These English rockets were brought over by many a Devonshire or Cornish woman to New England. They were also spelt rochet.

ROQUELAURE.

"Within the Roquelaures Clasp thy arms are pent
Hands that stretch't forth Invading Harms prevent."

In *A Treatise on the Modes,* 1715, a roquelaure is said to be a "short abridgement or compendium of a cloak, which is dedicated to the Duke of Roquelaure." These garments were worn by both men and women. The first mention I have chanced to see of one in New England is in the *Boston News Letter* in 1730, when one of Boston's citizens lost his "Blue Cloak or Roculo with Gold Buttons." Sir William Pepperell, who was a little shaky in his spelling, but possibly no more so than his neighbors, sent in 1737 from Piscataqua to one Hooper in England for "A Handsom Rockolet for my daughter of about 15 yrs. old, or what is ye Most Newest Fashion for one of her age to ware at meeting in ye Wint[r] Season." From 1736 to 1764 appeared, in the *Boston News Letter* and *Bos-*

ton Evening Post, such advertisements as these: "Cloth & Silk Roqualos," "Camblets for Roquelos of a peculiar color & Fabrick." The following roquelaures were all lost by careless folk: "Light colour'd cloth Roccelo that has a Double Cape;" "Blue Drab Roquelo napp'd within, has two capes to it;" "The person who borrowed some time since a Light colour'd Roquello of Mr. Richard Billings on the Town Dock is desired immediately to return the same to him." It may be noted that the correct spelling—roquelaure—is never once hit upon in all these liberal variations.

The variety of colors and materials described as worn in these outdoor garments give one a vivid idea of the gay appearance of town streets in New England throughout the middle of the eighteenth century. I do not find any universal use of the word in the South.

Roses. See Shoes.

Ruff. We usually associate bands, straight or falling, with the stiff-necked Puritans ; but ruffs were occasionally worn. The portrait of Winthrop shows a very neatly plaited one ; and he left fourteen " ruffes " by will. The portrait alleged to be that of Miles Standish, and dated 1625, shows also a ruff of fine proportions.

RUFFLES. When Richard Richbell, of Boston, died in 1682, he had seven pair of ruffles and ribbons worth seven pounds. Ruffles on shirt-fronts and at wrists did not go out of fashion for Boston beaux for a century after Richbell's death. In 1755 " Flowered Lawn Ruffles " and " Lace & Millinet for Gentlemens Ruffles " were advertised ; and the following year treble ruffles. Many portraits of this date show bosom-ruffles. Thomas Hutchinson's fine waist-coat has a ruffle from extreme top to bottom. The wrist-ruffles of Thomas Boylston's portrait (about 1760) nearly cover his hand. The portrait of Peter Fanueil shows him in velvet ruffles.

RUSSEL. A woollen cloth like baize much used in New England. It had a close-grained twill and was very durable. Manufactured originally of various weights, and made into various garments, it finally seemed to be assigned wholly to the manufacture of women's and children's shoes. See SHOES.

SACQUE. Fairholt says the sacque was a woman's garment introduced into England about the year 1740. This date seems to be widely incorrect, since Madam Pepys had "a French gown called a Sac" in 1669. The sacque worn during the last half of the eighteenth century was a flowing garment open in front, and sometimes drawn away in loops or plaits on each side. It hung loose from the shoulders to the ground in great folds over the hooped petticoat, and was universally worn by fashionable dames in old England and New England, and probably in the Southern colonies. In 1751 there were advertised in the *Boston Evening Post* "white calico with work'd sprigs for sacks," and "Rich Tobine & tissues for men & women's wear, chiefly Gowns and Sacks & worn mostly by the Gentry in England and France." The following year Elizabeth

Murray had for sale in Boston "Izavees Moorees & Humphumps for Sacks;" and a little later, "a large Sortment of Cloth coloured trimmings for Ladys sacks." In 1758 was lost a "Blue Damask Sack Gown with Close Cuffs laid with White Stuff most to the top." At a sale of a "great variety of womens apparel" in Boston, in August, 1774, were twelve rich sacks and petticoats. In the *Receipt for Modern Dress*, written at that time, we read:

Let your gown be a sacque, blew, yellow or green,
And frizzle your elbows with ruffles sixteen.

The fashionable colors for sacques in 1774 were "new palish blue or dark lilac satin." They were trimmed down the sides with chenille or blonde lace, often put on in waves or furbelows, and sometimes were richly lined. The fashionable materials were striped satin or tobine, but almost all other light silks or stuffs were used.

SAFEGUARD. The significant name of an outside petticoat of heavy woollen or linen stuff, worn by women over other garments to protect them from mud and mire, while the wearer rode on horseback. This was, of course, before the advent of the riding-habit. In the year 1600 Queen Elizabeth had thirty-one cloaks and safeguards, thirteen safeguards, and forty-three jupes and safeguards. New England women were usually satisfied with one apiece. In 1654 Ellinor Tresler, of Salem, left by will her "Sad collered Cloake, Wascote, Safeguard & Gouene to goe together"—an outfit such as we read of in the *Noble Gentleman*, "your safeguard, cloak and your hood suitable." Governor Winthrop sent a "gown, peticote and saveguard" to his granddaughter in Stamford in 1648. The name was used in England until this century; the garment is still worn there by farmers' wives; but I do not find it referred to in New England after the middle of the eighteenth century. Ann Warder wrote of the Quaker women of Pennsylvania in 1786: "They are very shiftable; they ride by themselves with a safeguard, which, when done with is tied to the saddle and the horse hooked to a rail standing all meeting time as still as their riders sit."

Other names for a safeguard were foot-mantle, as Chaucer wrote, and weather-skirt. And the "Manchester riding petticoat" seized by a Philadelphia sheriff in 1760 was a safeguard.

SAGATHY. Among "All Sorts of Winter Goods" advertised in the *Boston News Letter* of December 15, 1715, appear sagathies. In other notices it is spelt sagathees. It was a woollen stuff used chiefly for men's garments, and was said to be very durable. We read of a Philadelphia runaway in 1752 wearing off "a light cloth-colour'd Sagathy coat lined with Lead colour'd Allapine."

SAMARE. This garment was said by Randle Holme to be a sort of jacket for women's wear, with four tails or side laps reaching to the knee. Under various spellings—somar, simarre, simar, samarra, cimar, cymarre, and chymarre—it was applied to various over garments; and in a poetical sense, as by Scott in *Ivanhoe*, to a loose, flowing robe. Its original meaning was a *sanbenito*, or garment worn to execution by persons condemned by the Inquisition.

The garment, called a somar in the Salem tailor's bill, given on page 21, was a samare. I find the word used in New York in 1662, in the inventory given on page 26 of the rich wardrobe of the widow of Dr. Jacob De Lange. She had one silk potoso-a-samare with lace worth £3; one tartanel samare with tucker worth £1 10*s*.; one black silk crape samare with tucker worth £1 10*s*.; and three flowered calico samares worth £2 10*s*. As these samares were enumerated with the petticoats, and as no other jackets or doublets are named, it is evident that they were worn over the rich petticoats, and they were of materials of various weights for summer and winter use. In a Dutch dictionary, published in Amsterdam in 1735, a samare is defined simply as a woman's gown.

Sarcanet. This thin but firm silk, used under the same name to the present day, was made as early as the thirteenth century, and was also called sendal. It was also spelt sarsnet, scarsonett, and sarsinet, and was much used for cloak linings and for hoods, and appears in all lists of milliners and mercers.

SAY. Originally a silk material—soie. Spenser says: "His garment neither was of silke nor say." It came at a later date to be applied to a thin worsted stuff. Benjamin Franklin enumerated say with woollen stuffs, such as cloth, kerseys, serges, friezes, etc. I find "black Sudbury Say" advertised in the *Boston Evening Post* as late as July, 1768; and say appears also in the earliest New England inventories; twelve yards of green say were worth one pound and thirteen shillings in 1629.

SCALLOP. Pepys wrote in 1662: "Made myself fine with Capt. Ferrer's lace band, being lothe to mar my own new Scallop, it is so fine." In a Maryland trial at about that same date, the washing of a certain lace scallop bore an important part; but the word was rarely used in the colonies. A scallop was, as its name indicates, a collar or band scalloped on the edge.

SCARF. An article of dress worn by men and women, and forbidden to poor folk in Connecticut in 1676. Old Major Pyncheon had, in 1703, a "Trooping Scarff with Goold Lace" worth £3 10*s*. Furbelowed scarfs of gauze and net were worth one pound and thirteen shillings, and were worn by women of fashion.

SENDAL. See SARCANET.

SERGEDENIM. The name of a material, probably our modern denim. Advertised in the *Boston Independent Advertiser* of September, 1748, and in the *Connecticut Courant* of April 22, 1776, and thus spelled—searge de-nim.

SERGEDESOY. See DESOY.

SHADE. In 1755 it was advertised in colonial prints that "capuchins & shades" would be made to order. These shades were apparently a head-covering. On June 1, 1738, in the *Boston News Letter*, "Worsted Shades;" in 1753, "white Paris net shades;" and in 1755, "fine Flowered

Gauze for Shades"—were all advertised. The word shade in these notices was applied to a stuff rather than to head-gear or garments. Thus Eliza Southgate Bowne wrote, about the year 1800:

> If you see anything that would be light and handsome for our summer gowns I wish you would get them. Why cant you go and see McClellans Lace Shades. I think there are some for ten shillings a yard.

I do not find the word shade defined as a stuff in any dictionary, but in a poem printed in 1766 I find in a list of materials—

> Painted lawns and cheqer'd shades
> Crape that's worn by lovelorn maids,
> Watered tabbies, flowered brocades.

SHADOW. A shadow was a sunshade, either worn on the head or carried in the hand. In 1580, in England, a "Cale and Shadoe" were worth five shillings. We read, in *Purchas' Pilgrimage*, of "shadows to defend in Summer from the Sunne, in Winter from the raine." In the inventory of the estate of Richard Lusthead, of

Mattapinian, Md., in 1642, we find "plain shadows" among other headgear. They are also named in Virginian inventories.

SHAG. A heavy woollen cloth with a long nap, much used in New England, but possibly too heavy for Virginia and the Carolinas. Pyncheon wrote from Springfield for "tawny, murry, & liver-culler shagg." George Vaughan, a New Hampshire settler, received in 1632 ninety yards of shag at eighteen pence a yard. It was advertised in the *Connecticut Courant* as late as October 15, 1790. It was much used, to quote Carlyle's phrase, "for petticoats and other indispensable garments."

SHALLOONS. Peter Fanueil ordered, in 1737 shalloons at 4*s*. 6*d*. a yard. Phillips gave, in 1706, this definition of the material: "Shalloon, a sort of woolen stuff chiefly used for the linings of coats, and so called from Chalons, a city of France where it was first made." It was in texture not unlike our modern challis. I cannot find that the words and stuffs, though similar, have any direct connection. The name shallons appears in advertisements till this century.

SHAPE. A shape was originally a head-covering. In 1753, June 11, in the *Boston Evening Post*, "New Fashion Childrens Bugle & Silver Shapes" appear. Cotton shapes also were advertised; and in October, "Flowered Velvet Shapes, ditto in Various Colours cut & flower'd," which were either a stuff or a garment. In 1767 "New Taby Shapes" were "25 sh per piece." This meaning of the word shape, as given in all the eighteenth century newspapers, is entirely overlooked by the dictionaries.

SHAWL. The first notice that I have seen of the sale of shawls in America appeared in the *Salem Gazette* in 1784: "a rich Sortment of Shawls." This was at the time of the birth of the East India trade. The use of the shawl in Europe is practically of this century.

SHEEN-STRADS. See SPATTERDASHES.

SHERRY-VALLIES. A sort of pantaloon or legging worn on horseback, as a protection against bespattering mud, over trousers or breeches, and buttoned up on the outside of the leg. Rebecca Franks, writing in Revolutionary times, said of General Charles Lee, that he rode in "old green breeches patched with leather." He answered her with asperity that they were "actually legitimate sherryvallies such as his majesty of Poland wears, who let me tell you, is a man who has made more fashions than all your knights of the Meschianza put together." In a note in the *United States Magazine*, for January, 1779, it is said that "sherry-vallies were a kind of long breeches reaching to the ankle, with a broad stripe of leather on the inside of the thigh for convenience of riding." A Springfield tailor thus advertised in 1825:

> Shorrevals and Overalls
> And Pantaloons he'll make,
> Cutting too he'll always do
> And will no cabbage take.

These "shorrevals" were sherry-vallies.

SHIFT. The old English word shift was universally used by all English-speaking folk to denote the feminine under-garment now known as a chemise. Ann Clark and Jane Humphreys, settlers in Massachusetts in 1666 and 1668, left shifts by will. In 1738 Elizabeth Gedney, of Boston, had fourteen shifts valued at £8 4*s*. Madam Usher had "7 Holland shifts and 1 Flannel shift." Shifts appear in the inventories of men's estates, but were not, I think, ever worn by men.

Shoes. The Virginian planters stepped on the banks of the river James in boots; but the universal foot-covering of the Pilgrim and Puritan colonists was shoes. "Four hundred peare of shues" were ordered for the one hundred emigrants to the Massachusetts Bay Colony in 1628. Part of an order for these colonists was made according to this contract: "Agreed with John Heuson to make eight peare of Welt neates leather shues closed on the outsydes with a seam; to be substanciall good ouer Leather of the best and 2 soles, the Inner soale of goode neates Leather, and the outer of tallowed backs." "Dekers of the best bend Lether" were also carried to the new land for the purpose of making new shoes when these stout English ones were worn out, and a tannery was established at Ipswich, Mass., in 1634, to provide new leather.

Many of these shoes that were furnished to the early planters were thirteen inches long, and were not made with pointed toes either; on such sturdy bases did the founders of the new colony rest.

In Connecticut the leather-tanning and shoemaking trades were quickly established; and it is painful to know that the founders of a "state whose Desire was Religion and Religion alone," quickly learned to cheat in their shoemaking. As early as 1647 a large lot of the shoes made by the Connecticut colonists proved grievously poor and unworthy—the thread weak, the leather weaker; and lawsuits were quickly brought by the incensed shoe-buyers. When the matter was brought before the magistrates, Contractor Meigs tried to throw the blame on his workman. The latter in turn brought witnesses to prove that "Goodman

Meigs said to Goodman Gregory, Flapp them together, they are to go far inoughe," and so he (Gregory) did flap them together as ordered. The leather, too, did not prove to be as represented, and in order to avoid further deception the court decreed that "every Shoemaker in the town mark all those shoes he makes of neates leather before he Sells them with an N upon the lap with-inside below where they be tied." At the same date the finest shoes were marked, in comical contrast to our modern slang, "N. G."

In delivering final judgment on Goodman Meigs the court said: "In a single pair of shoes several evils appear: such as contempt of court, continewed unrighteousness, and other similar evils; and how many shoes he had made and sold of such faulty materials, and so loaded with evils the court say they know not." Thus was the depravity of inanimate objects rebuked by the Puritan magistrates.

It is common to represent the Puritans as shod with buckled shoes, but certainly these New Haven colonists wore shoe-strings instead of buckles. The latter are not mentioned in the early inventories, but shoe-strings were important enough to be left by will, as by that of Mrs. Dillingham, of Ipswich. Perhaps they were "rich spangled marisco shoe-strings," such as Dekker wrote of in 1633 in his *Match Me in London.*

If shoe-strings were valuable enough to be bequeathed, of course shoes would be also. William Replye, of Hingham, a wealthy man, left "one paier of shoes to my son" by will. Scores of other instances could be given.

Sizes were designated by numbers, as at the present day. From the inventory of the estate of Robert Turner, of Boston, in 1651, we learn that No. 11 shoes were worth 4*s.* 6*d.* a pair; No. 12 shoes, 4*s.* 8*d.* a pair; No. 13 shoes, 4*s.* 10*d.* a pair. In 1672 a law was proposed in Boston to prevent shoemakers from asking more than five shillings a pair for sizes 11 and 12. Laws were enacted in other communities to prevent extortionate prices. In Connecticut in 1676 shoemakers could have only "five pence half penny a size for all playne & wooden heeled shoes, and seven pence half-penny a size for well wrought French Falls.'' French Fall shoes, whatever they were, remained in style for some time. Runaway Indian servants were advertised in the *Boston News Letter* of October, 1711, and of September, 1713, as wearing French Fall Shoes. In Maryland this style of shoe seems to have been common wear as early as 1653.

The advertisements of runaways at that date show a vast variety of styles. One in 1712 wore "Square To'd Shoes with Steel Buckles;" another, in 1707, wore "Round to'd Shoes;" a third, in 1711, had a "New pair Wooden Heeled Shoes;" and, in 1716, one had "old shoes with strings in them." By 1723 low leather heels appear, and shoe-buckles of steel, brass, and silver, even on negro slaves. The Virginian slaves seem to have worn largely "Virginia-shoes." I find the name used for the wear of field-servants till this century.

Of women's shoes in the seventeenth century we know but little. Doubtless the

Puritan dames and maids followed closely the Puritan goodmen in shape and material of their foot-gear. Pointed shoes came in style by 1730, and, like those worn by English ladies of fashion, were of thin material. In 1740 "Mourning Shoes" appeared in the *Boston Evening Post*, and in April, 1742, in the same paper, Mrs. Nutmaker advertised that she had at the Three Sugar Loaves and Cannister "Womens fine Silk, flower'd Russel, white callimanco, Black Russel, Black Shammy, & Girls Flower'd Russel Shoes, Black Velvet, white Damask, & flower'd silk Clogs, Womens black & childrens red Morocco shoes and pumps;" a pretty variety, surely. These shoes were not at all cheap. In 1748, in the *Boston Independent Advertiser*, appeared this notice: "Greatest Variety of Beautiful Silk Shoes as has been imported in many years. Russel and Callimanco Shoes 52s 6d a pair;" and the silk and damask ones were higher priced still.

John Hoses shoes were great favorites for many years, and were sold everywhere throughout the colonies. In 1764 Jolley

Allen, the enterprising Boston shopkeeper, advertised "John Hoses shoes at 56s. Silk Shoes at 6s. Neat made Russel shoes at 47s 6d and Lyn made shoes at 36s." This last item brings us to a very important feature in shoe-wearing in America—the manufacture of shoes in Lynn. Shoes were made in that town as early as 1670—coarse shoes with straps and buckles — and the manufacture constantly increased. By 1750 women's shoes of fine quality were made with "white and russet bands closely stitched with waxed threads." The toes were pointed and heels were high, "cross-cut, common, court and wurtemburgh" heels. In 1763 best Lynn made shoes were advertised in Boston papers—"womens callimanco Shoes of all colours and sizes made by the neatest handed workmen in Lynn at 38s a pair and cheaper by the quantity." The manufacture of shoes in Lynn increased so in quantity and quality that it completely revolutionized the trade.

Women's shoes were made of still other materials than have been mentioned—damask, cloth, everlasting. Avis Binney had for sale in 1751 "womens best Damask Worsted shoes in fashionable colours, viz: Saxon blue, green, pink colour, and white;" so it is plain that very light-colored shoes prevailed at that date. In 1782 came on the brig Sally to Providence a large stock of "embroidered shoe Vamps" and "Sattinet patterns for Ladies' shoes of various colours with a set Flower in the Vamp." So we see that *women's* shoes disappeared with the Revolution, and with republican simplicity *ladies'* shoes came in. Low heels, too, made their appearance, no heels even, sandal-shaped foot-gear, about the year 1790. Very low heels had been advertised in the *Boston Evening Post* of 1764, but I fancy they were on servants' shoes. Children's shoes followed the fashions of their elders. Boys wore leather and kid, and little girls had "silk Damask, red moroco and flowered russel shoes."

All these vari-colored and vari-shaped shoes for women's and ladies' wear had thin soles. I have never seen a pair of century-old shoes, no matter what the material, with anything but "paper soles." Hence the vast sale and wear of clogs, goloshes, and pattens.

At intervals throughout the century buckles of different sizes and materials were worn on women's shoes, but it is impossible to give the exact dates of such wear. "Sorted Colours of Shoe Roses," as advertised in the *Salem Gazette* of July, 1784, had also their day, alternating with buckles and ferret shoe-strings in favor.

In the cases at the Essex Institute at Salem, and in the Museum of Art at Boston, in the rooms of the Worcester Society of Antiquity, and in the Deerfield Memorial Hall may be seen handsome shoes that were worn by women in the past century; high-heeled, pointed-toed, of as rich material as the gowns, they are broader in the sole across the ball of the foot than would now be considered elegant or graceful. See Batts, Brogues, Pumps, Slippers, Cockers.

SHOEPACK. A shoe shaped like a moccasin, without a separate sole, but made of tanned leather, and much worn in Revolutionary times.

Silk Grass. From the earliest years of the colonies until well into the eighteenth century I find constant references to a textile called silk grass. Mr. Eggleston says it was the "cotton" from the milkweed. This statement cannot be correct; the milkweed pappus was called silk-down. John Winthrop, in a letter to Sir Robert Murray in 1671, explains at length that the silk down from the "silke podds" was used to stuff beds and bolsters and for tinder; and he adds, "Concerning ye question whether it be spun, I have heard of some have tried it but never saw any but some grosly spun for candlewicke."

Many references vaguely indicate the real character of silk grass. On December 23, 1640, Thomas Georges wrote to John Winthrop for "some of that stuffe which with us supplies the want of hempe. Our Indians make theyr snow Shoes, nets and bags of it. Alsoe of a bigger stalke called silke grass which makes very fine hempe." Francis Higginson wrote in 1630 that there were in New England "two kinds of herbs that bear two kinds of flowers very sweet which they say are as good to make cordage or cloth as any flax or hemp we have." Some indication of its identity is found in the Travels of Kalm in Pennsylvania in 1744, who writes: "Instead of flax several people make use of a kind of Dogsbane or Apocynum cannabium. The people prepare the stalks of this plant in much the same manner as we prepare Hemp or Flax." Many other travellers and planters bear glowing testimony to these "herbes." Cartier speaks of them, calling them chanure (chanvre). Berkeley writes of them in Virginia. In the *True Relation concerning the State of New England*, 1634, we read of "three sortes of plantes whereof Lynnen & Cordage may be made, the coursest sort excells our hemp & the finest may equal the coursest silke." In 1628 "two tun weight of silke grasse" was ordered by the Massachusetts Bay Company; and Matthew Cradock, writing from London in 1629 to Endicott, said: "The like do I wish for a ton weight at least of silk grass." It was evidently used to weave with silk, for in 1719, in Judith Sewall's outfit was ordered "Good strong black Silk Damask, no Silk Grass to be in it." And we know Queen Elizabeth had a gown made of it. It must have been strong and tough, for I find it constantly advertised for sale for shoemakers' supplies. In the *Boston News Letter*, May 23, 1727, "Good Silk Grass Suitable for Cordwainers;" on December 26, 1728, "Very good Silk Grass for Shoemakers." Both cordwainers and braziers also had it for sale in Boston at the same date.

Skilts. Sylvester Judd, a most reliable and valued authority, thus described in *Margaret* this garment:

> Her father and elder brother wore a sort of brown tow trousers known at the time as skilts; they were short, reaching just below the knee, and very large being a full half yard broad at the bottom.

They were worn during Revolutionary times, and seem to have been a forerunner of trousers.

Skirt. The first application of this word in the sense of petticoat appears in 1768, thus: "Fine Flower'd Dimothies for Skirts." "Quilts for Ladies Skirts." Skirts of coats and waistcoats had been previously named. We read in the *Journal of a Young Lady of Virginia* (1782):

> Hannah was dressed in a lead-coulered habbit open, with a lylack lutestring scirt. Sister wore a blue habbit with a white Satin scirt.

SLEEVE. In the reign of Henry VIII. the sleeve was often a separate article of dress and the most gorgeous and richly ornamented portion of the dress. Outer and inner sleeves were worn by both men and women. But Elizabeth banished the outer sleeve, though she retained the detached sleeve. In our colonial days separate sleeves still were worn by women, but not such gay sleeves. A careful student of the history of the sleeve notes:

> The flat lace or linen collar of the early part of the seventeenth century had a depressing effect on the sleeve; it was still full, but flattened on the shoulder. It was not until the latter part of that century that the sleeve merely to the elbow became common in England; and the eighteenth century was emphatically the age of the elbow sleeve, with

its frills of real lace and ornaments of fluttering ribbons. In the days of the Revolution the sleeve vanished.

The " slytting " or slashing of sleeves was still in vogue in Pilgrim days, and was regarded as an idle vanity. Massachusetts men and women were forbidden to have more than one slash in each sleeve, nor could they wear sleeves over half an ell wide. Short sleeves, " whereby the nakedness of the arm may be discovered," were also prohibited, or were to be reinforced and made properly modest with linen cuffs. Existing portraits prove how little these laws were heeded. A double-puffed " virago " sleeve seems to have been much worn by women just previous to the assumption of the elbow sleeve. Few indications of the wear of detached sleeves are noted among the English colonists ; but Dutch women had almost universally a " pair of sleeves." Sometimes these were worth three pounds a pair. They were often trimmed with " great lace " or gold lace, and seem to have been a truly elegant and convenient fashion.

I wish to note, in passing, a definite use

of the word hanging sleeve, which I have not seen given in any of the dictionaries or histories of costume, which always characterize hanging sleeves as an ornamental oversleeve. It was often used by Pepys in his diary, and by Judge Sewall in his letters, solely to indicate a portion of the dress of a child, in fact to symbolize a dress of infancy. Judge Sewall also used it to indicate second childhood, thus, "I am come again to my hanging sleeves." A girl who was "still in hanging sleeves" was still a little child, not even a miss in her teens.

SLIDERS. See SLYDERS.

SLIPPER.

> Standing on slippers which his nimble haste
> Had thrust upon contrary feet,

wrote Shakespeare in his day. Henry VII. when writing to inquire the personal appearance of a princess whom he wished for a wife, asked if she "stood in slipers." Judge Samuel Sewall wrote to Edward Hall, in 1686, thanking him for "your loving Token the East India slippers to my wife;"

and in his diary, of his own footgear, "Going out to call the Fisherman in slip-shoes I fell flat." Randle Holme writes of slap-shoes—shoes with a loose sole.

Part of the lading of the Neptune, which was sold at Andrew Faneuil's shop or wharf in Boston, in 1711, were "slippers." Morocco slippers appear frequently for sale in the early American newspapers.

In 1796 Sally McKean wrote to the sister of Dolly Madison of the modes of the day:

> There have come some odd fashioned slippers for ladies made of various color'd kid and morocco with small silver clasps sewed on; they are very handsome.

SLIVERS. See SLYDERS.

SLOPS. The signification of this word has greatly varied. Originally a loose cassock for woman's wear, it came to mean a smock-frock, then a night-gown; then, in Shakespeare's time, it meant wide, full, Dutch breeches—knickerbockers—and such is its signification when used in old New England, though apparently for overall breeches to be worn to protect other breeches or hose. The old English application of the word to a certain form of shoes is not found in America. Its present colloquial use is to indicate cheap, ready-made clothing. The eighteenth-century word cantsloper, or khantsloper, used by Colonel John May, of Boston, in his diary, is in some obscure way related to the word slops, and meant—judging from its relative position in sentences—what we now term a mackintosh.

Slyders. The word slyder is given by Felt as a New Englandism for overalls. I have found it frequently so used in inventories of goods sent from England to Wynter at Richmond's Island in the years 1635 to 1640, and spelt slyders and sliders. Boys' "camnas" sliders, as well as men's, were invoiced to him, and were worth five shillings a suit. We read in the account of a shipwreck on the Florida coast in the early colonial days, that the men were cast ashore in slyders. Slivers, or slivings, were loose slops also worn by sailors, but do not appear to have been overalls.

SNAIL. See LACE.

SNOW-SHOE. In the Suffolk County Records of the year 1651 snow-shoes were named as part of Thomas Sautell's estate. One of the Winthrop letters, dated 1640, speaks of the Indians making the cords of their snow-shoes of silk grass. Josselyn, the traveller in New England, wrote in 1670, of "snow shooes made like a large Racket we play Tennis with." As late as 1748 they were called rackets. In 1704 it was enacted that the militia on the frontier be provided with snow-shoes, and all the colonists in outlying towns quickly learned to use them. At ordinations in Maine the visiting clergy often appeared on snow-shoes, and doctors visited their patients thus shod. Rev. Thomas Smith writes in his diary of a couple who came to him on snow-shoes to be married.

SOLITAIRE. "Bag wig, laced ruffles and black solitaire" were the marks of a man of fashion in 1760. The neck decoration called a solitaire was introduced in France in the reign of Louis XV. It was a broad black ribbon worn loosely around the throat, apparently to protect partly the coat from the powdered wig. Often it was tied to the back of the wig and brought around and tucked in the shirt ruffle. This fashion immediately preceded the large white bow of lawn and lace that was worn by the Macaronis. It was in high fashion in America, and solitaire ribbons were advertised in many American newspapers, especially in the Southern States.

SPATTERDASHES. In the *Boston Evening Post* of 1763 were advertised, "Thread and Cotton Spatterdashes." These were a covering for the legs to protect trousers, stockings, etc., from mud and wear. They were part of a soldier's uniform. The modern word spats is therefrom derived. Spatterdashes were also called copper-clouts, and sheen-steads, both English local names; and were also spelt spatterplashes. See SHERRY-VALLIES.

STAMIN. A heavy cloth like linsey-woolsey, or taminy, *q. v.*

STAMMEL. A woollen cloth, possibly called also stamin. It was like flannel and much used for petticoats; and being red, the name also was applied to the color red. We read in Hakluyt's *Voyages* of "carsies of all orient colours especially stammel," and also of sending for stammel dyes.

STARTUPS. This word is found in New England inventories of men's attire. Thomas Johnson, of Weathersfield, Conn., had a "perre of startups" in 1640. They were a sort of buskin or half-boot, for common wear. In Thynne's *Debate between Pride and Lowliness*, a countryman wears these shoes, which are thus described:

> A payre of startuppes had he on his feete,
> That lased were up to the small of the legge;
> Homelie they were, and easier than meete,
> And in their soles full many a wooden pegge.

STAYS. I do not know when "whalebone prisons" for women first were worn, but it is certain that many a pair crossed in the Mayflower and tight-lacing was known in the twelfth century. Stays appear in the early inventories of women's attire—as valuable heirlooms. In 1679, upon a Salem tailor's bill is the item, "To altering & fitting a paire of stayes 1s 6d." Whalebone at that time was worth 2s. 6d. a pound. By newspaper days, as early as 1714, we find advertisements of very good silk stays, and later of stay-makers:

This is to give notice to all Gentlewomen, Ladies & Other Persons who may have Occasion for New Stays that David Burnet from Great Britain who now lives near the Sign of the Ship upon the Stocks in Battery March, in Boston, makes all Sorts of Stays after the Newest Best Fashion, And also makes Stays for such as are Crooked or Deformed in their Bodies, so as to make them appear Strait, which was never before done in this Country.

Stay-maker Burnet may be held responsible, for at least forty years, for Boston dames' wooden, flat figures which he trussed up in "turned stays, jumps and gazzets," and finally in caushets—which I suppose was the provincial way of spelling corsets. I have also seen the word "coascetts" in a seventeenth-century inventory. In New York and Philadelphia stays were made and sold.

Women's stays and "custulls" are advertised in the *Boston Evening Post* in 1761; but if David Burnet knew what custulls were, we do not, nor gazzets either.

We also catch many a glimpse of the materials of which stays were made. Thus, on January 12, 1767, William Palfrey at the Heart and Crown had an "Assortment of Stay Trimming consisting of Fine & Coarse Yellow Holland, Galloun, Strapping braid & cord, White Sattinet, Stay Tick, Best White Watered Tabby, White and half Stiffened Buckram, White Bellandine Sewing Silk."

Good specimens of old-time stays can be seen in the cases of the Essex Institute and the Deerfield Memorial Hall—real iron-clads—with heavy busks and adamantine bones, and covered with stiff buckram. I have been told frequently of *tin* stays, but have never seen them.

STAYHOOKS. These hooks were not to fasten stays, but were small and ornamental and to be stuck in the edge of the bodice to hang a watch or étui upon. The first offer of them for sale which I have seen is in the

Boston Gazette in 1743. "Silver'd Stay-hooks," and "silver stayhooks with fine stones." In the *Boston Independent Advertiser* of August, 1749, appears this notice: "There was taken up Yesterday a Hook for a Womans Stays. The Person who lost it may have it by enquiring of the Printer." In 1762, on June 7, the *Boston News Letter* contained the advertisement of "Gold & Stone Sett Breast Hooks, Plain Stay hooks and Stone sett Ditto." These were pretty trinkets, and were in high fashion for many years. I have seen in old jewel-boxes several stay-hooks much resembling our modern chatelaines; there are one or two preserved in the cases of the Essex Institute. Since they were more frequently of silver or hard metal than of gold, many have perished with the century.

STIRRUP-HOSE. See HOSE.

STIVERS. Edward Skinner, who died in 1641, named in his will "1 Payr fustian Stivers and 1 Payr leathern Stivers."

STOCK. See NECKSTOCK.

STOCKINGS. See HOSE.

STOMACHER. Bishop Earle wrote thus of Puritan garb and "she precise hypocrites" in 1628: "A nonconformist in a close stomacher and ruff of Geneva print, and her purity consists much in her linen." A stomacher is sufficiently defined through its evident derivation—a band or ornamental girdle worn over the stomach. They have been in fashion at varying intervals until the present day, and have been made of many and varying materials—folded silk, orris, leather, silvered gimps, beads, spangles, and, as shown in the *Boston Evening Post* of November, 1755, of "Bugle and Pasteboard." In the *Pennsylvania Gazette* of July 24, 1760, we read of "gauze and bugle stomachers with floss flowers." A writer in the *Weekly Rehearsal* of January 10, 1732, complains of the variation in the fashions of stomachers, saying, "sometimes it Rises to the Chin, and a Modesty-Piece suffers the purpose of a Ruff, again it is so Complaisant as not to reach Half-Way." Abigail Adams, writing to Mrs. Storer, in 1785, says she encloses "patterns of a stomacher, cape and forebody of a gown; different petticoats are much worn, and then the stomacher must be of petticoat color."

STRIP. An ornamental portion of dress apparently solely for women's wear, and used to cover the neck or breast. We read in *Penelope and Ulysses*, 1658,

> A stomacher upon her breast so bare,
> For strips and gorget were not then the weare.

Among the rich possessions of one Richard Lusthead, of Mattapinian, Va., in 1664, we find "9 laced stripps, 2 plain stripps." They were evidently an elegant piece of apparel.

SURDAN. In the *Boston Gazette and Country Journal* of June 13, 1774, a runaway slave was advertised as wearing a "blue Surdan," which was apparently a jacket or waistcoat.

SURTOUT. A great-coat for men's wear, or an outside sleeved jacket for women's wear. We read in the *Boston Gazette* of

February 6, 1769, that there was lost "Last Monday Ev. two very good plain & Knapt Bath Beaver Surtouts of a light mixt Colour one very large the other suitable for a Boy of 12 years." In letters of that same date we read of travelling mantua-makers coming to make cloth surtouts for all the daughters in the family.

SWANSKIN. Fairholt says swanskin was a thick fleecy hosiery. But from early days we read in American newspapers of runaways in swanskin jackets, and also of "Ell-wide Swanskin for Ironing cloth," which would seem to point to its being a cheap fleecy cloth like Canton flannel.

TABARET. This advertisement from the *Boston Gazette* of 1749 somewhat defines this material: "Worsted Tabaritts the newest fashion. In Imitation of a rich Brocaded Silk." It was a sort of poplin, and was much used for petticoats, and later, of slightly heavier make, for upholstering purposes. Tabbinet was a similar material with a watered surface.

TABBY. A plain soft silk. It was advertised for sale in the *Boston News Letter* as early as October, 1711, and was a favorite material for women's wear. It varied much in value. A petticoat of tabby was worth, in 1660, £2 10s. We read under date 1676 of "1 Pair Tabby Bodyes cloath colour'd ½ wide & long wastied." Within a hundred years the name has been applied to watered silks. We find Peter Faneuil's sister sending word to England to have an old gown dyed and "watered like a tabby." See TOBINE and TABARET.

TAFFETA. This was not originally our modern plain silk called by the name, but was in Chaucer's day a heavier, costlier silk. Ann Hibbin's taffety cloak was, from its value — £2 10s. — of rich quality. The name was also applied to thin linen.

TAMINY. A woollen stuff glazed like alpaca, made in Norfolk. It was spelt also tammin, tammy, tamin, etaminee, and estamine. I learn from the accounts of John Pyncheon, of Springfield, in 1653, that "red Tammy" was worth at that date 2s. 10d. per yard. Martha Emmons, who died in Boston in 1666, owned a red tamminy petticoat; one of her neighbors had a "taminy wast cote." I find tammy and taminy advertised in Connecticut newspapers as late as 1775. The "mixt Estamains" worth eighteen shillings a yard, that were sent to Deliverance Parkeman, in Boston, in 1703, were also taminys.

TEWLY. See TULY.

THERESE. A large veil or scarf worn as a head-dress, usually of a light, thin material, such as gauze or mull. Thereses were worn toward the close of the seventeenth century, and are named in the lists of New England milliners.

THUMB RING. See RING.

TIFFANY. A thin gauzy silk. Tiffany hoods were forbidden to folk of modest fortune by the early sumptuary laws of Massachusetts, so must have been deemed rich wear. Tiffany was frequently advertised in

Boston newspapers; in 1739, in the *News Letter*, and spelt "Tifyny;" in 1741, in the *New England Weekly Journal*, and spelt "Tiffeny." It appears so frequently with crapes and cypress, that I think black tiffany must have been much used in mourning wear, indeed almost appropriated to that use.

TIPPET. A narrow covering for the neck. In 1763, November 6, in the *Boston Evening Post*, Jolley Allen advertised "Mecklenburg Tippets for Women & Children;" and on January 11, 1767, he had "very Gentell Tippets Silver'd at 22s 6d." Gauze tippets were advertised also. William Palfrey had blue and silver, and white and silver tippets. Rattlesnake tippets were of fine blonde stuck with flowers. All these were ornamental additions to the toilet; but in the winter tippets of various kinds of furs were worn for warmth. The *Weekly Rehearsal* of January 10, 1732, comments on the tippet as "an elegant and beautiful Ornament; in Winter the Sable is Wonderful Graceful & a fine Help to the Complexion."

TOBINE. A heavy silk material much used for rich gowns and sacques. In 1742 the *Boston News Letter* advertised "Silk of Sundry Sorts as Rich Tobine." Striped and flowered tobins were named, and "Tobine Lustrings at 9 sh sterling a yard," and "Rich tobine and Tissue for men & womens wear chiefly gowns and sacks." For men's wear it was used in waistcoats—the striped seeming to be the favorite. It was akin in quality to tabby, *q. v.*

TONGS. Loose trousers or overalls of linen or cotton stuff. In *Margaret*, by Sylvester Judd, we read, "The boys were dressed in tongs, a name for pantaloons or overalls that had come into use." The word was not in common use at the time of the Revolution.

TROLLOPEE. A loose gown like a negligee, worn during the last half of the eighteenth century.

TROUSERS. The first hint of anything like the use of the word or article trousers, appears in the items of consignments to John

Wynter, of Richmond's Island, Me., in 1638. "7 pair of trushes £1 1s." The word frequently appears in his later accounts and is always thus spelled. These "trushes" were probably tow overalls for the use of Wynter's fishermen, though slyders, which were overalls, were also named. Trouses, trossers, trews, and trusses were other early forms of the word. Through newspaper items we learn of runaway slaves wearing off "chequer'd," tow, or ozenbridge trousers, sometimes over their breeches. One was advertised in the *Weekly Rehearsal* of September, 1733, as wearing "Cinnamon colourd Plush breeches with Trousers over them." Another in the *Boston Gazette* of May 27, 1771, is said to have run off in "Buckskin breeches and white trousers." It seems evident that the word was at first applied to a garment of the nature of overalls. A contemporary writer thus describes them: "linen drawer trousers which are breeches and stockins all in one and fine cool Wear." One servant who ran off in knee-breeches was "reported to have been seen later with Frock and Trowsers on."

These tow trousers were also called tongs. Sailors wore trousers. The portrait of Teach, the pirate (called Blackbeard), shows him in trousers. The date of portrait is about 1734. Trousers did not come into general wear till after Revolutionary times; in fact, not till this century. The first mention I have seen of woollen trousers was dated 1776. See TONGS, SLYDERS, SKILTS.

TUFFTAFFETA. This stuff was a taffeta with velvet or plush tufts of nap or raised pile. I have never found any tufftaffeta garments named save in New England inventories, and then only jerkins and doublets for men—no women's wear.

TULY. Also tewly. A color—red. "To make bockerum tuly—a mannor of red colour, as it were of crop madder." I read of tuly waistcoats in New England.

TURBAN. In 1763 "Silk and Tinsel Turbins" were advertised in the *Boston Evening Post*, as early an advertisement as I have noted of turbans. In 1767 the *Connecticut Courant* advertised a box containing a "turbant and tippets." Silvered gauze turbans were very fashionable and were frequently trimmed with feathers. Until well into this century women wore and had their portraits painted in turbans, which, when made of rich materials, were a truly imposing headgear.

Though I have never seen turbans advertised for men's wear, there are many portraits in existence of masculine New Englanders wearing turbans, or a headgear closely resembling the feminine turban. The portrait of Edward Bromfield, and those of Thomas Boylston, Thomas Hubbard, and Master John Lovell in Memorial Hall in Cambridge, all display caps much like turbans.

UMBRELLA. Though umbrellas are mentioned in Quarles's *Emblems* (which was printed in England in 1635) and by various English authors after the year 1700, they were not used in the colonies till after the middle of the century. In the year 1740 a belle in Windsor, Conn., carried an umbrella which had been brought to her with other elegancies for the toilet from the West Indies. Her neighbors mocked her by carrying sieves balanced on broom-handles. By 1762 they were advertised in Boston papers by all enterprising and modish milliners, and by other tradespeople.

Among the earliest special advertisements of umbrellas is this from the *Boston Evening Post*, June 6, 1768:

> Umbrilloes made and sold by Isaac Greenwood; Turner, in his shop in Front Street at the following Prices. Neat mahogany frames tipt with Ivory or brass ferrils 42s 6d plain; others at 40s; printed at 36s; neat Persian Umbrellas compleat at 6 10s and in proportion for better silk. Those Ladies whose Ingenuity Leisure and Oeconomy leads them to make their own may have them cut out by buying Umbrella sticks or Forms of him; and those Ladies that are better employed may have them made at 15s a piece. N. B. All the above Prices are in O. T.

Oliver Greenleaf likewise advertised in the same paper the same year, on May 23d, "very neat Green and Blue Umbrellas." Another Boston man, "Unmade Setts of Sticks for Umbrilloes for those who wish to cover them themselves."

The early spelling was usually "umbrilloe" and "umberaloe." The shape, can we judge from the newspaper wood-cut, was very flat, with few ribs. The old umbrellas seen in museums are very heavy of frame and very large.

VAMPAY. Sometimes spelled vamp, or vampay. A short woollen hose, or stocking, reaching only to the ankles. One advertisement of a runaway servant described him as wearing knit vamps. Another wore knit boots over his hose, which boots were probably vamps.

VEIL. These shields for the face were worn by Puritan women, and were enjoined by Roger Williams. But Minister Cotton proved that such wearing was not commanded by the apostles, and veils were discarded by Salem and Boston dames in 1634—so runs the tale.

VEST. In Pepys's time the word vest meant "a long cassock close to the body," which was not necessarily a sleeveless garment like a waistcoat. It seems curious while I have never seen the word vest used in New England, either in print or manuscript, until the middle of this century, that it was constantly used in Pennsylvania in the previous century. From the newspapers alone innumerable examples can be given. In the *Pennsylvania Gazette* of May, 1752, we read of runaways wearing off stocking-wove vests, with coats, showing that these vests were waistcoats. In the same publication, under date of January 13, 1729, another runaway wore a corded dimity vest flowered with yellow silk; and on June 30, 1736, one wore a cinnamon vest-coat, which sounds like a Tony Weller pronunciation. See WAISTCOAT.

VIZARD. See MASK.

WADMOL. Originally weadmel, a coarse heavy stuff made of Iceland wool, and brought from Iceland to Suffolk and Norfolk, England. It came to mean a very coarse, felted woollen stuff. We read of "wadmoll mittens," of "a woadmell petticoat." The name does not appear later than the year 1700. And I have never seen it in inventories of the Southern colonies.

WAISTCOAT. A term used in early days, as now, for an undergarment reaching from the neck to the waist, and usually sleeveless. In 1628 each Bay emigrant had two "wascotes of greene cotton bound about with Red tape." The Piscataquay planters had red waistcoats supplied to them. Women and men both wore them and left them by will. Edward Skinner, in 1641, in Boston, and Martha Emmons, in 1664, had "wastcotts." Jane Humphrey had them in variety of kersey, serge, and fustian—green, white, gray, blue, and "murry collured." It took "4 yardes and halfe a quarter of tuft Holland" to make Lawyer Lechford's wife a waistcoat, which is much more than would be necessary for a simply shaped waistcoat nowadays. Widow Oxenbridge, of Boston, had white dimity waistcoats. In 1721 knit "westcots" were advertised in the *Boston News Letter;* in 1767 "Damascus Lorettos & Burdets for fine westcoats," and "fine Rich Pink colour'd Vellure Silk for waistcoats" were also sold. "Knit Maccorini waistcoats" and waistcoat patterns also appear in the list, among the latter "the Sportmans fancy, the Prince of Wales Newmarket Jockey, the Modest pale-blue." In the early part of the eighteenth century the waistcoat became an important article of attire, being very long, as displayed in the portraits of the founder of Yale College, of Sir William Pepperell, Sir William Phips, and other gentlemen of their day. It was low in the neck, however, showing the cravat all around the neck; it was richly embroidered or trimmed with great gold or silver buttons and laces. Sir Charles Frankland said in 1763 that seven yards of gold lace were needed to trim a waistcoat.

WATCHET BLUE.

"The saphir stone is of watchet blue."

In the early colonial days this word occurs, though rarely. It was defined in old-time words, "celustro, azure, watchet, or skie-color."

WEATHER-SKIRT. See SAFEGUARD.

WHISK. A neckerchief for women's wear, which was plain or laced, and fell on the shoulders; hence also called a falling-whisk. It was apparently formed at first simply by turning the ruff down. We find Madam Pepys buying a white whisk in 1660, and later a "noble lace whisk."

A whisk was not common or cheap neckwear. The same year that Madam Pepys wore her whisk to court, Governor Berkeley, of Virginia, paid half a pound apiece for "Tiffeny Whisks." I think they were a cavalier elegance, for I have never seen the name in use but once in New England. Wait Winthrop, in 1682, sent a whisk to his niece Mary.

WHITNEY. A heavy and rather coarse cloth in universal use in the eighteenth century. To show its value, let me state that Peter Faneuil ordered from London in 1737 "Fine Whitneye at 53s a yard, Coarse Whitneye at 28s a yard." Its color was commonly scarlet. It was used for coats, jackets, petticoats, breeches, and extensively for cloaks. It was also spelled Witney.

WHITTLE. This was a double blanket worn by West country women over the shoulders like a cloak. The word was derived from the Anglo-Saxon *hwitel*, and is found in *Piers Plowman*. In 1655 Mary Harris, of New London, left a "rred whittle" by will, and Jane Humphreys, of Dorchester, had, in 1668, "a whittle that was fringed." A whittle was apparently much like a shawl. The name became obsolete in the eighteenth century in America, but was frequently used in England till a much later date—in fact, may still be heard.

WILDBORE. We read of "Marone Ribb'd Wildbores" in the *Salem Gazette* of 1784, and the name appears frequently elsewhere, until this century. Wildbore was apparently a heavy repped woollen goods, and was much used for women's winter gowns.

WIG. From a very early date wigs were in fashion in the colonies. As early as 1675 the legislature of Massachusetts felt it necessary to denounce wig-wearing. But the question of the propriety of donning wigs was a difficult one to settle, since the ministers and magistrates themselves could not agree. John Wilson and Cotton Mather wore them, but Rev. Mr. Noyes launched denunciations at them from the pulpit, and the Apostle John Eliot delivered many a blast against "prolix locks with boiling zeal," but yielded sadly to the fact that the "lust for wigs is become insuperable."

Wigs were termed by one author "artificial deformed Maypowles fit to furnish her that in a Stage play should represent some Hagge of Hell;" by another, "Horrid Bushes of Vanity;" and other choice epithets were applied.

Governor Barefoot, of New Hampshire, wore a periwig as early as 1670; only seven years after Pepys first donned one.

In 1676 Wait Winthrop wrote to his brother in New London:

> I send herewith the best wig that is to be had in ye countrye. Mr. Sergeant brought it from England for his own use and says it cost him two guin-

eyes and six shillings, and that he never wore it six howers. He tells me will have three pounds for it.

The Winthrops frequently ordered wigs, and their portraits display some full-blown ones.

By 1716 the fashion of wearing wigs had become universal; though in 1722 at a meeting at Hampton a remnant of sturdy Puritans passed a resolution that "ye wearing of extrevegant superflues wigges is altogether contrary to truth." In 1730 the Assembly of New York placed a tax of three shillings on every wig or peruke of human or horsehair mixed, and even Pennsylvania Quakers cut their own hair and wore wigs. When I read of these wig-wearing times, and of the grotesque and mountebank wigs that were worn, I wonder afresh at the manner in which our sensible ancestors disfigured themselves.

In the *Boston News Letter* of August 14, 1729, we read:

Taken from the shop of Powers Mariott Barber, a light Flaxen Naturall Wigg Parted from the forehead to the Crown. The Narrow Ribband is of a Red

Pink Colour. The Caul is in Rows of Red Green & White.

Grafton Fevergrure, the peruke-maker at the sign of the Black Wigg, lost a "Light Flaxen Natural Wigg with a Peach Blossom-coloured Ribband." In 1755 the house of barber Coes of Marblehead was broken into and eight brown and three grizzle wigs stolen; some of these must have been absurd enough, with "feathered tops," some were bordered with red ribbon, some with three colors, pink, green, and purple. In 1754 James Mitchell had white wigs and "grizzles." He asked 20*s*. O. T. for the best. We read of the loss of "a horsehair bob-wig," and another with crown hair, and a goat's hair natural wig with red and white ribbons. Wigs were also made of "calves tails," and the *Virginia Gazette* advertised, in 1752, "Mohair stain'd" for wigs. Thread and silk were also used.

Hawthorne gave this list of wigs:

The tie, the brigadier, the spencer, the albemarle, the major, the ramillies, the grave full-bottom, and the giddy feather-top.

To these we can add the campaign, the

neck-lock, the bob, the minor bob, the bob major, the lavant, the vallaney, the drop-wig, the buckle-wig, the Grecian fly, the peruke, the beau-peruke, the long-tail, the bob-tail, the fox-tail, the cut-wig, the tuck-wig, the twist wig, the scratch, the macaroni toupee. Sydney says the name campaign was applied to a wig the fashion of which was imported from France in 1702. This date cannot be correct, for we find John Winthrop writing in 1695 for "two wiggs one a campane, the other short." A campaign wig was made very full, and curled eighteen inches to the front. It had "knots or bobs a-dildo on each side with a curled forehead." The portrait of John Winthrop displays an enormous wig, perhaps this very "campane."

The Ramillies wig had a long plaited tail, with a big bow at the top of the braid and a smaller one at the bottom.

Wigs were of varied shapes. They swelled at the sides, and turned under in great rolls, and rose in many puffs, and hung in braids or curls or clubbed tails, and then shrank to a small close tie-wig that vanished at Revolutionary times in powdered natural hair and a queue of ribbon, a bag, or an eel-skin.

From the portraits of the day—those of Copley, Smibert, Blackburn, and Gilbert Stuart, and also of earlier artists—displayed in Harvard Memorial Hall, in the Library of the American Antiquarian Society, in the rooms of the various historical societies, a very correct sequence of wig fashions can be obtained, and dates assigned to certain shapes. The portraits of Virginians show some specially handsome wigs.

All classes wore wigs. Many a runaway slave is described as wearing off a "white horsehair wigg," a "flaxen natural wigg," or a "full goatshair wigg." A soldier deserter in 1707 wore off a "yellowish periwig," and as a specially absurd instance of servile imitation, I read in the *Massachusetts Gazette* of July 11, 1774, of a negro who "wore off a curl of hair tied on a string around his head to imitate a scratch wig." Just picture that woolly pate with its dangling curl!

The account books of Enoch Freeman, of

Portland, Me., contain in 1754 such entries as this:

Shaving my three sons at sundry times	£5. 14s.
Expense for James Wig	£9.
Expense for Samuels Wig.	£9.

The three sons were Samuel, aged eleven, James, aged nine, and William, aged seven. Imagine any father in a small town being such a slave of fashion as to have the heads of little sons shaved and bedecking them with such costly wigs.

At the beginning of this century women, having powdered and greased and pulled their hair almost off their heads, were glad to wear wigs. At first "tetes" of curled hair were donned, as early as 1752; then came "locks." We find Eliza Southgate Bowne when a young girl writing thus to her mother from Boston in the year 1800.

> Now Mamma what do you think I am going to ask for?—A WIG. Eleanor Coffin has got a new one just like my hair and only 5 dollars. I must either cut my hair or have one. I cannot dress it at all stylish. . . . At the Assembly I was quite ashamed of my head, for nobody had long hair.

Wigs were bequeathed by will. Robert Richbell, of Boston, left eight by bequest; so also did rich Philadelphians. The cost of dressing and caring for wigs became a heavy item of expense to the wearer, and income to the barber; often eight or ten pounds a year were paid for the care of a single wig. Governor Hutchinson had a formidable annual barber's bill. Wig-maker's materials were expensive also—"wig ribans, cauls, curling pipes, sprigg wyers, and wigg steels," and were advertised in vast numbers.

391.0973 Ea7
00806389
STACK
Costume of colonial
3 5049 00159 7562
GT607.E2 1974